SELF-CARE JOURNAL

Your wellbeing has never been so important. We need to take care of ourselves both physically and mentally, and do so without guilt. The *Self-Care Journal* is here to nurture both your physical and mental health through interactive mindful prompts and tasks that will help you to reflect on your life. Explore positive journaling, intention setting, and positive habits, as well as how to find sustainable happienss in life. Discover how to add gratitude journalling to your every day and think about random acts of kindness that will make both you and others feel great. Take care of yourself through exercise, healthy eating, and creative activity. The main goal of this journal is to encourage you to be mindful of your wellbeing every day by creating positive habits, which is strengthened through 66 days of journaling.

FOX CHAPEL
PUBLISHING

ISBN 978-1-64178-172-5

Fox Chapel Publishing makes every effort to use environmentally friendly paper for printing.

For more information about the Future plc group, go to *http://www.futureplc.com*

Future PLC Team
Editor: Rebecca Greig
Designer: Katy Stokes
Compiled by: April Madden & Briony Duguid
Senior Art Editor: Andy Downes
Head of Art & Design: Greg Whitaker
Editorial Director: Jon White
Written by: Zara Gaspar, Rebecca Lewru-Gray
Cover images: Getty Images

Fox Chapel Publishing Team
Managing Editor: Gretchen Bacon
Design and Production Manager: David Fisk
Copyeditor: Christa Oestreich

We are always looking for talented authors and artists. To submit an idea, please send a brief inquiry to acquisitions@foxchapelpublishing.com.

Printed in China
First printing

CONTENTS

WILD SPIRIT
soft heart
SWEET SOUL

A NOTE FROM THE EDITOR

ESTABLISHING A POSITIVE ROUTINE IS THE FIRST STEP TO BETTER SELF-CARE, BUT IT'S SO IMPORTANT THAT YOU DON'T LOSE SIGHT OF YOUR ORIGINAL INTENTIONS

There is a growing movement to prioritize taking care of ourselves—both physically and mentally. With so many stressors in life, our self-care has never been more important.

It can be very easy to isolate ourselves from friends and family. Whether getting too caught up with work or spending too much time on the internet, many of us feel adrift or unable to reclaim the opportunities we lost. When I moved across the country, I was away from so many people I knew all my life and wasn't sure how to start over. Big events in our lives or in the world can have an impact on how we move through our day, even if we don't realize it.

I'm lucky, though, because I had already established a mindful routine of sorts. I have written a journal every day for the past four years and had already explored a lot about mindfulness and mental health. Starting a personal journal wasn't an entirely conscious decision, but I started keeping one where I write about my day, thoughts, feelings, and aspirations. I try to keep it in the moment, and in general only reflect on the very recent past and ponder about the imminent future.

I naturally retain a lot of information and memories, and journaling has given me the chance to unload so much clutter from my brain onto paper. It's been vital in helping me to process my thoughts, reflect on my feelings to nurture mental self-care, and find mindfulness.

We can't necessarily choose what information our brains retain, but we can choose not to dwell on certain emotions, and we can train ourselves to let go. There are so many things in life that we can't control, which makes us feel helpless, anxious, and in some cases, angry. But sometimes the key to moving forward is accepting that there are things outside of our reach—and we should focus our energy on the things we can control.

When facing some tough times, I had a reasonable idea of what I needed to do to take

care of myself. I already had the routine of writing in my journal and knew from personal experience that I had to keep moving and occupied. I kept up my daily journal, even on days that I had nothing new to write down. Then I created a routine of activities: I walked to the beach each day no matter the weather, cooked from scratch often, lost myself in yoga and home workouts, and did a creative activity each weekend.

In maintaining this routine, however, I exercised too hard and temporarily lost sight of my wellbeing, which resulted in needing an MRI on my hip and being ordered to take it easy. The lesson here is simple: Once you have created a positive routine that works for you, be careful not to push it too far, and remember to check in with yourself regularly. Don't adopt habits that might ultimately be damaging, and try not to set yourself with unrealistic goals.

This journal is here to help you figure out what works best for you and to hopefully help you to create positive habits that benefit your mental and physical health. We'll look at different types of journaling and encourage you to think about a routine as well as things that will help you really take care of yourself.

Rebecca Greig

START WITH NUMBER ONE

SELF-CARE IS A SKILL. WITH THE RUSH OF MODERN LIFE IT IS VERY EASY TO FORGET THE VESSEL IN WHICH YOU LIVE, SO TAKE SOME TIME TO RECHARGE

SELF-CARE IS FOR EVERYONE

It is easy to fall into the trap of thinking self-care is all about hot baths, laziness, and treating yourself. It is important to remember that self-care can take the form of tending to your physical, emotional, social, financial, and personal needs. Self-care can also be exercised in both work and home spaces as well as in your everyday spirituality. Don't be fooled into thinking that you need to spend money to take care of yourself. Self-care is for everyone and can take many forms; what works for others may not work for you.

SELF-CARE CAN BE WORK

Self-care can be as simple as paying your bills on time or setting up automated payments so you don't have to worry about them in the future. Self-care can also take the form of keeping your surroundings clean, healthy, and comfortable. It's not always going to be things that you want to do, so take a moment to clear your work area—it's a form of self-care!

SELF-CARE ISN'T SELFISH

We shouldn't use self-care as an excuse to lie in bed all day, or to eat nothing but chicken wings. We use self-care as a way of looking after our mental and physical health. In a way, you're asking for what you need, not what you want. Self-care doesn't have to be introspective either; you could organize a regular call with someone close to you and be fully mindful of how you enjoy it.

SELF-CARE IS PERSONAL

There isn't a one-size-fits-all approach to self-care, and it means so many things to lots of different people. It's important to take a moment or two to work out what refreshes you, energizes you, and is effective (without being damaging), then embrace what helps you feel like the best version of you.

WHERE TO START

HERE ARE SOME SMALL WAYS TO BEGIN YOUR SELF-CARE JOURNEY. YOU DON'T HAVE TO START BIG BY CUTTING OUT SUGAR OR TRAINING FOR A MARATHON; SMALL CHANGES ARE THE BEST WAY TO BEGIN

HEALTHY SNACKS

Fuel your body with food that nourishes your body and soul. Choose whole foods and feed yourself regularly. An irregular eating routine is not the way to go for self-care. Eat colorfully, as the widest range of nutrients can be found in colorful natural foods. Avoid sugar, too— while it's tempting to reach for sweet comfort foods when you're feeling low, try to treat yourself kindly with a delicacy that will keep you going, rather than lead to a sugar crash. However, if you feel you really need something sweet, opt for a piece of dark chocolate. Dark chocolate boosts your endorphins, the chemical that is released to cope with pain, as well as containing antioxidants.

Remember to eat mindfully on occasion, eat without distractions, and focus on your food. Try to drink enough water, as thirst can often be mistaken for hunger, and adequate hydration is important for proper brain health.

GET CREATIVE

Creativity is a key part of what makes us human. While you may not think you're a creative person, there are many ways to flex your creativity and engage in some self-care at the same time. If you're really stuck on where to start, think back to what you enjoyed doing as a child —could you spend hours building things? Alternatively, what weren't you allowed to do as a child? As an adult, now is your opportunity to get messy or to make something big for your home. Art and creative projects don't need to have a clear focus or end goal. Play with your materials and let your mind wander. Don't let yourself fall into the trap of feeling like everything you do needs to be productive; there is immense value in creative pursuits. When being creative we're using a different part of our brains than in everyday activities. Challenge yourself by doing something creative that you've never tried before—pick up an adult coloring book or try a musical instrument!

READ POSITIVELY

The world out there is often a very scary and negative space. We are bombarded with news stories that inform us of things that are outside our control and only serve to depress us. This kind of stress is unnecessary and often leads to sleep loss as well as a feeling of helplessness. Mass media floods our days and is often a source of motivation, but if not used carefully it can take over and prevent us from living to our fullest!

Instead of waking up and going straight to social media or opening your news app, start your day with something positive, such as an inspiring book or motivating podcast.

The words that we choose to consume are part and parcel of the way that we view the world. If we go looking for the negative and bad parts of media, very often this is all that we see. Instead of focusing on the negative stories, search for positive influencers and you'll find your mindset changes too.

BE NICE

Actions speak louder than words, but intentions matter, so take a moment to remind yourself to do something for others. Acts of kindness, such as helping out other people, also help to make us feel better about ourselves. Reflect on a time when a stranger did something that brightened your day—how did that make you feel? Does it make you want to be the cause for that kind of positivity for others? Offer a helping hand to those in your family and friend group. Send care packages as a way to remind those you love that you're thinking of them!

Actions as simple as smiling at a stranger or letting someone have a turn ahead of you can make the world of difference to someone. Remember that we never know the private battles other people are going through. When you radiate kindness you're putting positivity out into the world with your actions.

MEDITATE

Meditation has been around for thousands of years and can take many different forms. While it may at first feel a little awkward to begin meditating, you're taking part in a practice that has its roots in the Latin word, which means "to ponder." Meditation in all its forms is pretty common and doesn't have to have a religious or spiritual angle if that isn't your thing. Mindfulness grew out of meditation and can help people who experience anxiety or depression. One of the key elements of meditation is to be in the moment, paying attention to our bodies and our breath. When clearing your mind, it's important to be kind and gently guide yourself back to the exercise. Find a place where you are comfortable and will not be disturbed—this is time for you.

EXERCISE

While you're caring for your emotional, intellectual, and spiritual sides it's also important to care for your physical self. There's no better way to make yourself feel worse about a situation than to just sit and obsess over it. Your mind is focused on the negatives, and you can't think of anything else. Instead of simmering, get up and get moving so that your endorphins start pumping.

Many people call exercise the ultimate form of self-care as you are improving your body and showing yourself what you can do when you put your mind to it. Regular exercise is important for a healthy mind as well as a healthy body. Exercise improves self-confidence, reduces stress levels, and has the brilliant side effect of improving your sleep, too. While it often feels difficult to make time for both exercise and self-care, remember that the two come hand in hand.

JUST SAY NO

While it might sound incredibly negative, saying "no" is actually one of the greatest forms of self-care. You are taking into consideration what your time is worth, and what you really want in the long term. In all self-care practices, it's important for you to look out for what is truly best for you; for example, an extra doughnut might feel like a treat in the short term, but how are you going to feel about it once the sugar high is over? By saying "no" to a request or demand, you're emphasizing your personal boundaries. You're also learning to prioritize what is truly important and what is actually urgent. Your energy is a finite resource, and you can't say "yes" to people at the expense of your own self-care.

UNPLUG

Tech: we can't live without it. But we can control the dose we give ourselves. It's all too easy to open your emails or unlock your phone to do one little task, only to find ourselves with five new things we've taken on—often forgetting our original purpose!

Try to be more intentional with what you're using your tech for. Put down the phone when you've checked the time. Log out when you've clarified that one point in an email. Most importantly, focus on using your tech for good. Try to avoid negative websites or articles that you know will upset you. Take a day to do a digital detox and be mindful of what you notice when you aren't plugged in! Of course, we cannot live without being connected all the time, but try to be more aware of how and when you use tech. What does it help you achieve, but also what does it prevent you from doing to the best of your ability?

YOU GOTTA NOURISH TO FLOURISH

MAKE A SELF-CARE COMMITMENT

Under each topic make a list of self-care activities that you could do for yourself. They can be as small as drinking an extra glass of water or as big as taking a full day to yourself for some pampering.

Relaxation ....

....

....

....

Expression and creativity ....

....

....

....

Health ....

....

....

....

Companionship ....

....

....

....

Now, make a commitment. Plan when you will make time for some of these activities.

Every day I will . . .

Once a week I will . . .

Once a month I will . . .

WELLBEING IS BEING WELL

WE'RE ALL LOOKING FOR WAY FOR SELF-CARE BE HAPPIER. IT'S TIME TO LOOK INWARD TO WHAT YOU REALLY NEED BOTH MENTALLY AND PHYSICALLY TO FOR SELF-CARE

Wellbeing is personal to everyone, and the general make up of what wellbeing consists of is subjective; it's something that is unique and personal. Your perfect state of wellbeing will be totally different to your friend's. Wellbeing also needs to be understood by the different constituent parts that make it up: spiritual, emotional, physical, social, economic, and intellectual. Therefore, wellbeing is both physical and mental, and we function more effectively when we are both mentally and physically happy and healthy.

Many people may feel that self-care is a new "catchall" to encourage us to buy more products or classes to "improve" our wellbeing, but it can be as low cost as you need it to be. In short, your wellbeing is stable when you can cope with the challenges that life throws at you with the resources you have. Life is a balancing act and so is self-care; when you feel that you're running out of resources to meet your challenges, you don't feel at your best. Likewise, if you're feeling like you're coasting with no challenges, you may feel sluggish and your wellbeing stagnates.

When we work on improving our wellbeing, we can give ourselves goals. Even if you don't achieve your goal, you can take the opportunity to reflect on why it didn't work out. Did you set yourself a goal that was too exhaustive? Try to choose a few small ways to improve your wellbeing every week. Anchor your intention to a time of day so you don't forget—put the time aside and enjoy looking after yourself. This intention could be something as small as a to-do list, or even a nap!

Of course, your mental and physical health changes throughout your life. It's important that you work to keep a happy and comfortable medium. In looking out for your mental and physical care, you can track any changes that may occur to you over days, weeks, or even months. You can start to recognize triggers or sensitive areas, and you can learn to mitigate them before you even come up against the issue. In this sense you're learning more about yourself and taking care of yourself.

Your perception of your wellbeing is affected by many factors, like your past experiences, past traumas, and your attitude. You may feel a certain way about what you deserve or the way you "should" look after yourself. While you cannot change what has happened to you in the past and how you've reacted to them, you can change your current attitude and the way you approach your future. Self-acceptance is key for self-care, whether this is mental or physical.

WHAT IS WELLBEING?

The very dry, dictionary definition of "welbeing" is the state of being comfortable, healthy, or happy. This can, and does, relate to anything to do with health, comfort, or happiness, so it's pretty broad. Our mental health is how you look at the world, how you feel about yourself, and how you deal with life and the challenges it sometimes presents to us all.
Looking after our wellbeing ensures we're confident, active, and happy.

There is so much that can be done to improve our physical and mental wellbeing. Your health should be a top priority; ensure you get enough exercise, a balanced diet, and enough sleep and rest. These kinds of healthy behaviors are key; after all, we cannot separate our mind from our body; it's all connected. Keep your body active and you may find that you look for more opportunities to be active.

Likewise, look after your mental health by keeping your brain challenged with new hobbies. It's important to be creative too; we can use creative pursuits (such as drawing, knitting, singing, painting) to distract us from stress, preventing us from cyclical thinking or dwelling on the thing that worries us. Taking our mind off a problem, while seeming counter-intuitive, often helps us solve the problem—our brains are working away in the background while we focus on the task at hand! When starting a new hobby there is nothing like the sense of achievement when you finally "get it." That's a real mood booster! You may also make some new personal connections when starting a new hobby.

If all this wellbeing practice sounds exhausting, you should also ensure that you make enough time for relaxation. You are not a machine. Everyone needs time to decompress and occasionally do absolutely nothing of "value." Resting is important for your health too!

Your health, both mental and physical, can be improved by connecting with others. Whether this is offering help or asking for it, human connections nourish us. No one is an island. We give and receive great positivity through our relationships.

GET IT DOWN ON PAPER

So many of us had a teenage diary, a place to let out all your confusing feelings and frustrations. A journal is a more grown-up version of this. We express ourselves through our journals, helping us track what stresses us out and making a permanent record of what is good in our lives too! Keep journaling simple, write a little bit every day, and don't beat yourself up if you forget a few times. Treat your journaling as a bit of you-time and unload—remember you don't have to share any of what you write with anyone else.

WHAT'S ON YOUR MIND?

LET YOUR MIND WANDER AND USE THIS PAGE TO WRITE DOWN ALL OF YOUR THOUGHTS AND FEELINGS RIGHT NOW

TRANSFORM THE EVERYDAY

WE ALL HAVE ROUTINES, WHETHER WE REALIZE IT OR NOT! WHEN YOU LOOK TO CHANGE UP YOUR ROUTINE, AS A ROUTE TO WELLNESS, YOU CAN ENCOUNTER DIFFICULTIES IN STICKING TO IT

Routines are incredibly useful in helping us feel in control of our lives, staying focused, and reducing our stress levels!

WRITE IT ALL DOWN!

Journaling is a great way to help you stick to a new or amended routine. You can use brain dumps to unload your day or use checklists and daily trackers to ensure you're working through your new routines. Checklists keep us on track as no one likes to break a successful chain of habits!

We can also use our journal to ensure all the parts of our life are balanced. Life is a balancing act, and acting on autopilot means we forget to pay attention to key parts of our life; your home life may suffer if you prioritize work too much, and vice versa. You'll also raise your self-confidence when you take notice of how much you achieved in one day.

MAKE IT REALISTIC FOR YOU

There is no point in creating a brand-new wellness-focused routine that won't work with your real life. If you simply don't have the time to craft a holistic dinner every night, don't make it part of your routine! You'll only set yourself up for failure and feel defeated. Start by making small changes; in the example of dinner, make it a goal to add more vegetables in your bowl—this is really easy to make routine, and soon you won't even think about it!

MAKE IT FUN

Adding mindful activities to your routine doesn't have to mean living like a monk. If meditation and breathing work sound terribly serious, try to add a dash of fun to your daily routine! Use music to energize yourself, laugh about nothing, or take a moment to think about past memories that make you smile and take note of your body's reaction. Life is for living, and by enjoying your time mindfully, you will find your outlook remains sunny; you may also find yourself being more resilient in the face of challenges.

JUST LIKE CLOCKWORK

In starting a new routine you need to take stock of what is important to you. Prioritize what you want to include and break it down into small goals. Get prepared with any materials you may need; there is no point in committing to a healthy-eating routine when you haven't been grocery shopping. Start small and work regularly on your new routine. If possible, try to stick to similar times; pretty soon you won't have to expend conscious effort on your new routine—it'll just happen! If you need a little more of a push, think about any reward you can give yourself when you hit a milestone or set amount of days/weeks/months to stick to your routine.

KEY POINTS OF THE DAY

Mindful routines can be slotted into every and all parts of our days. When crafting a new or amended routine, turn your expectations upside down and start with your bedtime routine. This may seem a bit backward, but in reality, you're starting your day the night before, setting yourself up to succeed with your actions even before you sleep! Instead of feeling rushed in the morning, looking for the right clothes, set them out the night before, prep your breakfast, and pack your bag ready to leave the house. Turn off technology early and ensure you get a quality amount of sleep—you'll sleep better knowing so much of your morning routine is already in motion!

Mornings can be a rush, but if you keep your routine simple, you can stick to a more mindful morning. Almost anything can be done mindfully, but some routines do lend themselves to greater mindfulness; drinking your morning hot drink can be a meditation and a ritual in itself. Focus on your senses and appreciate what's in your mug.

Mindful "check-ins" can be undertaken at any time in the day. Often lunchtime is a good time to check in with yourself and your daily experience. Play a little sense game with yourself to reconnect; what are three things you can feel, hear, and see? We can easily become distracted when we go through our daily routines, seemingly on autopilot. Try to use these tasks, whether washing the dishes or checking your emails, to practice mindfulness and keep your attention on the here and now.

BE KIND, ALWAYS

Often when we look to create or amend a routine, we fail. We have the highest expectation of ourselves, and this can set us up to fail, which in turn makes us feel worse! One of the key things about mindfulness is to be conscious of what is happening without judgment. It's important to treat ourselves with kindness when we slip up, as we're only human and life often gets in the way of our best intentions! Instead of beating yourself up over a perceived failure, take a moment to refocus. Remind yourself of your intention and work on making a positive action. Tomorrow is always another day. Be kind to yourself.

DECLUTTER YOUR DAY

Creating a routine is important if you want to look after your wellbeing. To make sure you are including things that are good for you, first declutter your everyday habits. Make a list of things you can remove from your everyday and another list of things you definitely want to include.

Things I want to remove from my routine . . .

Things I want to include in my routine . . .

MAKE A HABIT, BREAK A HABIT

OUR BRAINS NEVER FORGET OLD HABITS (THIS IS WHY WE CAN ALWAYS RIDE A BIKE, EVEN IF IT'S BEEN YEARS SINCE YOU WERE LAST ON ONE), BUT WE DO FAVOR NEW HABITS OVER OLD ONES

WHAT IS A HABIT?

Habits are, essentially, shortcuts for your brain. They're efficient, as you're automating actions and your brain can focus on other stuff! Whether you know it or not you've been training yourself to do certain tasks by rote and in response to cues. Now, your brain doesn't know the difference, chemically, between a "good" habit and one that is "bad" (like biting fingernails or a social media addiction), and frustratingly, "pleasure-based habits" encourage the release of dopamine (our brain's happy chemical). We crave dopamine and so we are rewarded to do the habit again! We can use mindfulness to change the habits we consider bad and help ourselves stick to the good habits we want to foster.

BREAKING BAD HABITS

Work on becoming more mindful when taking part in your habits (whether "good" or "bad") and how they make you feel about yourself. You will find that, at its most basic, our brains follow a pattern—trigger, behavior, reward. So we can use mindfulness to dig a little deeper into the "trigger" part of the pattern and we can turn off the automatic part of a habit. We can start by asking ourselves "Why?" when a bad habit rears its ugly head. Breathe fully to remind yourself to be present. If you find your mind wandering, or if you talk to yourself unkindly, bring yourself back to the task at hand with kindness; you're not looking to beat yourself up, but to better understand yourself. Why and what are you feeling when you reach for a certain habit (pattern of behavior)? Is it comfort you're looking for? How would you reroute this desire to something more healthy?

TRY LONGER THAN YOU THINK

We've long thought that it takes 21 days to form a habit. If you've ever been unable to sustain a habit after that "magic number" is passed, don't fret! The study that started this misconception was undertaken in 1960! In 2009 a group of researchers from University College London found that it takes between a month and nearly a year to form a habit properly. The average amount of time it took for a habit to stick was around 66 days. So keep sticking to those habits—it will take longer than you think to make them your new reality.

MINDFUL HABITS

There are reams and reams of positive habits that you can take up, whether to improve your day-to-day or to replace the bad habits you've fostered! There are also a vast array of mindful habits to adopt. Remember to start slowly and not rush to adopt all the mindful habits at once—that would only serve to set you up to fail, and feelings of failure are not what we're looking to cultivate!

Break your habits into the physical: feel your environment, breathe deeply, be mindful when eating. Emotional: practice being grateful, cry if you need to. Intellectual: listen to your intuition, speak kindly to yourself and others. And creative: read, when you create (food/art/anything!) take note of the sensations you experience.

Remember a key component of mindfulness is to live in the here and now. Be aware of the real nature of what you are experiencing. Work on fully living and enjoying your new habits. Be kind to yourself and remember that life changes quickly; what works for you one month may not work a few months later.

WRITE IT DOWN!

A key technique in helping ourselves stick to the new habit is to journal them. Write your intention down—what are you looking to achieve and why? The "why" can help you if you find a habit isn't sticking—what's your end goal? Remind yourself of it mindfully. Habit trackers are also incredibly helpful in journaling good habits—or even the bad! Instead of noting a long list of "things I must remember to do," make a chart with the date at the top or side and your list of to-dos on the other; you can then color them in if you hit your habit (or color in if you break a habit that day). Take pleasure in filling out your tracker; keep an eye on how your mood changes when you complete a full row of colors. Use your favorite colors or change them every month to keep it interesting visually!

IF AND WHEN YOU FAIL

There are many strategies you can use if you fail at sticking to a habit; and you will—you're only human! Our habits can be broken down by difficulty level and it's important to be kind to yourself. Remember, one day missed doesn't matter; work on not missing two days!

FINDING IT HARD?

While it can take between 18 and 250 days to form a new habit, there are a group of people that it may feel even more difficult for. Many people are "habit resistant." It's important to be kind to yourself if you feel like this may be you. Changing behaviors is tricky, especially if you're beginning a habit that is hard work to stick to, like a difficult exercise or trying to stop a "bad" habit.

DO YOU ALREADY HAVE HABITS?

USE THIS SPACE TO WRITE ABOUT THE THINGS YOU ALREADY DO THAT YOU WOULD SAY ARE GOOD AND BAD HABITS

My current bad habits are . . .

My current good habits are . . .

The positive habits that I would like to add to my day-to-day are . . .

POSITIVE POWER

YOU CAN'T ALWAYS CHANGE YOUR SITUATION, BUT YOU CAN CHANGE YOUR MINDSET. CHOOSE TO SEE THE GLASS AS HALF FULL NOT HALF EMPTY, AND THE POSSIBILITIES ARE ENDLESS

WHY IS POSITIVITY IMPORTANT?

Positive thoughts lead to positive outcomes. Studies have shown that a positive outlook can not only help you be happier, but can also benefit your wellbeing and result in positive actions.

FIND HAPPINESS

If you wake up each day with a positive mindset and a can-do attitude, your day will naturally start off better than if you begin the day with negative thoughts. If you dwell on the negative then nothing will change, but focus on the positive and good things are more likely to happen.

FINDING LONG-TERM HAPPINESS

Positivity is not always easy, especially because of how fleeting happiness can be. When something good happens to us, we tend to celebrate and then forget. However, when something bad happens, we dwell on it. Luckily, you can make small changes to your life to build sustainable happiness. Retail therapy provides short-term pleasure, but investing in experiences that give you a sense of accomplishment or purpose will keep you feeling positive for longer. Learn to appreciate the little things, make genuine connections with others, and be present in every moment of life. Instead of mulling over the past or worrying about the future, live in the moment and you'll be much more content.

EVERY

cloud

HAS A

silver lining

IMPROVE YOUR HEALTH

Focusing on the positive can help improve your mental and physical health. Research shows that an optimistic approach to life can not only help you manage stress levels, but also build up your immune system, making you more resistant to colds, aiding cardiovascular health, and even increasing your lifespan. People with positive attitudes tend to get more activity, choose healthier diets, and are less likely to smoke because their outlook makes them feel better.

ACHIEVE YOUR GOALS

Studies show that positivity improves performance and productivity. If you lie on the couch feeling sorry for yourself, you're unlikely to get a job. But if you focus on the positives and make a list of things you can do, such as taking a class for skills training, you'll feel more motivated. Those with a positive attitude tend to excel because they work to overcome obstacles and believe success is possible.

GIVE YOURSELF A TALKING TO

Self-talk is one of the biggest battles people face when trying to be positive. How you talk to yourself is crucial. We tend to build things up in our head and make scenarios worse than they actually are. If you're trying to lose weight but eat a chocolate bar, instead of getting angry with yourself, think about how you would talk to a friend if they were in the same situation. You wouldn't shout at them. You'd tell them to not be so hard on themselves. Talk to yourself how you'd talk to others and you'll start to feel more positive. Give yourself time, be patient and kind. You don't have to be perfect. Tell yourself you can do it. Eventually you'll start believing your own positive words.

START SMALL

Changing your mindset isn't easy, especially if things aren't going well, so don't take on too much at once. Write a list of all your negative thoughts and remember the "Rule of When." Stop telling yourself you'll be happy when you meet someone, find a job, or get fit. You can be happy now and still work on achieving those goals. Then, focus on just one thing, taking small steps. If you want to get fit, don't sign up for a marathon. You'll pile too much pressure on yourself and may feel worse if you fail. Instead, work slowly toward your goal, whether that's taking the stairs instead of the elevator or getting off the bus a stop early.

PRACTICE POSITIVITY

To practice positivity you need to be mindful of it. There's no point waking up with a positive attitude in the morning if you end up miserable by the afternoon. Stop throughout the day to think about whether or not you've tackled what you're doing positively or negatively. It's also important to practice activities that make you happy, and surround yourself with positive people. Get at least 30 minutes of exercise a day, read, meditate, have some "you time," talk to a friend, laugh, smile.

APPRECIATE LIFE

Write down three things that you're grateful for every day. This can be difficult when you feel like nothing is going right but, even if it's as minor as feeling the sun on your face, recognizing and remembering positive experiences will lift your spirits. We tend to remember the negatives, but if we write down the positives, we can remind ourselves that actually there's a lot to be grateful for. Don't expect positivity to happen overnight. It will take practice, but you'll get there.

BEWARE OF TOXIC POSITIVITY

While it's important to have a positive mindset, we can't be happy all the time and we shouldn't feel the need to deny or dismiss our emotions. Toxic positivity is when you or others attempt to be positive regardless of the situation. Phrases such as "Stay positive," "It could be worse," or "Happiness is a choice" can be toxic because they may make someone feel guilty about their emotions. When everything is going wrong, it's okay to be sad or angry. If you don't acknowledge your feelings, it will be harder to get over them, and you may not receive the support you need from others. Having a positive outlook doesn't mean you're never negative. All our emotions are valid. We should be allowed to feel whatever we're feeling, whether it's the loss of a parent or a job. The difference is that we don't dwell on the negative and, where possible, we focus on moving forward.

POSITIVE JOURNAL

EVERY DAY BRINGS A COMBINATION OF GOOD AND BAD EXPERIENCES, AND WE ALL TOO OFTEN FOCUS ON THE BAD THINGS, FORGETTING THE GOOD. MAKE A POINT TO RECOGNIZE THE POSITIVE EXPERIENCES NO MATTER HOW SMALL—RECORD THREE POSITIVE EVENTS AT THE END OF EACH DAY

MON

1. ....

2. ....

3. ....

TUE

1. ....

2. ....

3. ....

WED

1. ....

2. ....

3. ....

THU

1. ....

2. ....

3. ....

FRI

1. ....

2. ....

3. ....

SAT

1. ....

2. ....

3. ....

SUN

1. ....

2. ....

3. ....

CONSIDER KEEPING THIS UP EVERY EVENING. REMEMBERING THE POSITIVES WILL HELP TO KEEP YOUR MOOD BOOSTED

POSITIVE EXPERIENCES

WRITE ABOUT TIMES WHERE YOU HAVE DISPLAYED EACH OF THE FOLLOWING QUALITIES

COURAGE

KINDNESS

SELFLESSNESS

LOVE

PASSION

WISDOM

HAPPINESS

DETERMINATION

OWN YOUR FEELINGS

NEXT TIME YOU BLAME SOMEONE FOR MAKING YOU FEEL A CERTAIN WAY, REMEMBER THAT ONLY YOU HAVE THE POWER TO CONTROL YOUR EMOTIONS

YOU ARE RESPONSIBLE FOR YOUR EMOTIONS

Eleanor Roosevelt once said: "No one can make you feel inferior without your consent." When someone upsets us and we feel sad, angry, embarrassed, or disappointed, we tend to blame them for how we are feeling with exclamations of "He made me feel stupid," or "She made me feel like a nobody." If, for example, someone calls you dumb, you can choose to let it upset you or you can take charge of your emotions. They can't control how you're feeling if you don't let them.

Whether or not the insult is merited, how you feel about it is down to you. Instead of blaming others to justify the way you're feeling, it may be time to look inward. The only way to change is to take responsibility for your emotions. The next time something makes you sad or angry, look at the situation. You can choose to admit that you are sad or angry about what has happened because of your beliefs and expectations, then look at actions you can take to remedy this; or you can blame someone else and stay sad or angry for longer. Either ignore the insult or, if it's a friend, admit to them that maybe you're not as smart as them, but their words made you sad. Ask for their support instead of getting angry. It's likely they'll show you more sympathy and you'll feel better instead of feeling sad about the situation. Owning your feelings will not only help you feel happier sooner, but it will help you cope better in difficult situations.

EMBRACE ALL THE FEELS

We may spend our lives searching for happiness, but learning the importance of feeling all of our emotions is part of the journey. If someone dies you need to grieve; if you don't get a promotion you are allowed to be annoyed. It's important not to ignore your emotions; let yourself feel sad, angry, and annoyed. The harder you resist your feelings, the longer they'll stay with you. Many of us have grown up with people telling us, "Be a man," or to "Stop being a crybaby," but these phrases aren't helpful. The more you bottle up your feelings, the more likely they are to build and erupt on you, making things much worse.

CULTIVATING SELF-AWARENESS

Often, instead of acknowledging our feelings, we avoid them. We might eat to forget that we are sad about not losing weight, work all night when we're stressed, obsessively clean, or avoid being alone in order to escape what we are really thinking about. Stop telling yourself to just get over it, it's not important, or it's in the past, and instead deal with your emotions. Once you're aware of the real reason you're avoiding your feelings, you can process them and move forward.

BE SELF-AWARE

The first step to owning your emotions is being aware of them. Ask yourself how you're feeling, recognize what it is that you're feeling, and explore those emotions. Are you angry or is it a stronger feeling of betrayal? Are you stressed or just annoyed? The better you understand your feelings, the better you can tackle them. Let your emotions flow through you. Whatever you're feeling will pass.

BE KIND TO YOURSELF

When dealing with your emotions, remember that there are no wrong feelings. We might all wish we were happy all the time, but don't make happiness the goal. Focus on the now and let yourself feel every emotion. It's OK to fail; don't be too hard on yourself. Be kind.

TALK IT OUT

It's always good to have the support of your friends and family, and talking about your feelings can help you work through them. If you're really struggling, you could always seek out a counsellor or therapist to talk to.

WRITE IT DOWN

Journaling is also a great way to work through your emotions. Write down how you think someone made you feel. For example, "They made me feel so angry because they didn't listen to me." Then below, readjust your thought process. Write down how you can own your feelings, such as "I felt angry because they wouldn't listen to me, but they can't control how I feel. I will keep calm and tell them they need to listen to my point of view."

WHEN TO SEEK HELP

While it's important to feel different emotions, sometimes it's more than just sadness. It's fine to have a few days moping on the couch because you're sad that you didn't get that promotion, but depression is a different story. There are a number of ways to spot if it's time to seek help. Are you feeling hopeless, are you not sleeping or sleeping all day, are you unable to focus or enjoy your usual activities? Do you have mood swings, thoughts of self-harming, significant changes in your appetite? Are you using drugs or alcohol to suppress your feelings? If you don't have support and can't seem to see the light at the end of the tunnel, it's time to get help.

LET'S FOCUS ON YOU

WHAT CAN YOU DO OR CHANGE IN ORDER TO FOCUS MORE ON YOUR WELLBEING?

LET IT GO!

LEARNING TO ACCEPT THE THINGS YOU CAN'T CONTROL WILL NOT ONLY HELP YOU SEE THE BIGGER PICTURE, BUT IT'LL ALSO LIFT A WEIGHT OFF YOUR SHOULDERS

LEARNING ACCEPTANCE

Life doesn't always turn out the way we plan it. Whether your marriage has just ended or you get into a car accident, the unexpected can strike at any time. Life is unpredictable and at times unfair, but regardless of who is at fault, you can't change the situation. What you can do is control how you feel and react to it. Learning to accept what you can't change will not only help you find peace, but it'll also open up new opportunities.

LOOK AT THE BIGGER PICTURE

If you spend your life worrying about whether or not things could have turned out differently, you're just going to exhaust yourself. Instead, look at the bigger picture. If you've had a car accident, worrying about what you could have done to avoid it isn't going to change the fact that it happened. Look at the facts and identify your fears. Maybe you're worried your boss will fire you if you're late for work as a result of the accident, or that you can't afford the repairs. Instead of focusing on the worst possible scenarios, try to look at the situation from a different perspective. Consider whether your thoughts are based on fact or opinion. Your boss will likely understand why you're late, and at least you aren't seriously injured. You can't change the fact that you had an accident, and inventing disaster cases is not going to make the situation better.

MAKE IT HAPPEN

When you accept what you can't control and focus on changing the things you can, you'll not only find yourself in a more positive place, but you'll feel less worried, you'll have more energy to focus on the things you love, and you'll have a greater appreciation for them. Seeing things from a different perspective will open up new opportunities, you'll feel happier because you're not putting so much pressure on yourself to be perfect, and, in turn, good things will happen to you.

CHALLENGE YOUR THOUGHTS

It may be a good idea to make a list of the things over which you have control (how you feel and respond) and then a list of what you can't control (the ice on the road, how your boss is going to react, and the cost of the damages). Then make a list of what you can influence. You can speak to your boss and explain what happened, you can work harder over the next few weeks to make up for lost hours, or you can speak to the other driver. Your boss will probably be sympathetic and the other driver may decide not to claim on the damages. But until any of this has happened, it's best to focus on what you can control and let go of what you can't. Stop distorting things in your head and make a plan of how to manage your stress.

A *negative* MIND WILL NEVER GIVE YOU A *positive* LIFE

SEARCH FOR THE POSITIVES

You may feel overwhelmed or upset, but you can't beat yourself up when things go wrong. Maybe you didn't plan to be single at 30, but you need to stop thinking about what you expected from life. Instead, focus on what you want from it and how you can achieve your goal. Be aware of when you are trying to control the situation or other people. Were you holding on to your relationship when it had been over for years? Learn to let go of the past and grow from the experience. Of course, this doesn't mean you can't be angry or sad. You need to grieve the loss of your partnership, but you're not alone. Everyone goes through hard times and you will get through it. Don't compare yourself to others. A couple may look happy but you don't know what goes on behind closed doors. Instead, look for the positives and take advantage of what you can change. If you don't want to be single, get out there so that you can meet new people. Perhaps you want to enjoy your newfound freedom? Go travelling or take up a new hobby. This change could be a new opportunity and may bring about some unexpected joys too. You can do whatever you choose to do. You just have to make it happen.

SELF-ESTEEM JOURNAL

MON

Something I did well today ....

Today I had fun when ....

I felt proud when ....

TUE

Today I accomplished ....

I had a positive experience with ....

I helped someone by ....

WED

I felt good about myself when ....

I was proud of someone else when ....

Today was interesting because ....

THU

I felt proud when ....

I made someone's day better by ....

Today I had fun when ....

FRI

Today I learned ....

Today I was successful at ....

I felt proud when ....

SAT

I made someone's day better by ....

A positive thing I witnessed ....

Today I had fun when ....

SUN

I felt proud when ....

I felt good about myself when ....

I was proud of someone else when ....

BEST INTENTIONS

WE ALL SET GOALS. BUT GOALS CAN BE DIFFICULT TO ACHIEVE IF WE VIEW THEM AS AN ENDPOINT AND NOT AS A MANIFESTATION OF ONGOING CHANGE IN OUR LIVES

WHY SET GOALS?

In short, goals help you stay focused. Everyday life is full of noise and a seemingly never-ending list of things that need to get done. We all know how easy it is to get distracted with small jobs that crop up screaming for attention, and then the larger pieces of work (without deadlines) get missed. In fighting those fires, we lose sight of what is really important.

Often it can feel like your "must-do" list is cluttered with things that aren't helping you grow. When we set a goal, and achieve it, our self confidence grows and we find ourself progressing toward that ongoing change we're committing to.

When we set goals, we can also map out our steps to achieve the result we're looking for; this helps keep us on the right path and we also meet the deadlines we set ourselves. When setting a goal (and an intention) we're also being accountable—use these as a reminder to stick to it! If you wish you can also share your goals and intentions with people close to you (or at the very least, show others what we're focusing on). As well as helping us with accountability, unexpected sources may give us some extra help.

MILESTONES

When setting a goal it can be helpful to section the goal our into bite-sized pieces (usually giving yourself a month per milestone). For example: if your goal is to run a marathon before you turn 50, your intention may be "Running keeps me fit and healthy and happy." Your intention approaches the goal as if you've already done it! Your goal can then be easily broken down.

I AM CREATING THE LIFE OF MY *dreams*

TERMS FOR GOALS

A short-term goal is something to shoot for in the near future (generally under a year) and can be anything from journaling everyday, waking up a little earlier every morning, networking more, cutting your debt, or organising your work desk regularly! We use short-term goals for quick wins and quick feedback—you can see very easily if your methods are working. Long-term goals are a future accomplishment, they usually require lots of planning and are normally achieved a few years in the future. Try to stick with one long term goal; setting too many can lead to not achieving anything! If the difference between a long or short term is still a little fuzzy, think of your long term as a lifelong dream—there's no realistic way to achieve this in a week, so don't beat yourself up if you haven't given that TedTalk by next month!

KEEPING POSITIVE

Our emotions impact our performance at work, school, and at home. When we use goals and intentions we're staying positive in what we wish to achieve, and we're also setting out easily digestible steps, setting ourselves up not to fail but to succeed!

It is important to remember that stumbling on your goals shouldn't feel like a personal failure. We're all human and it is important to treat ourselves with kindness; mindfully reflect on what caused the "failure" and how you can turn it around—could you have prepared more thoroughly? Did you get distracted with other projects? Keep digging down into the why and you'll find the root cause of the problem. If you find yourself spiraling, take a moment to breathe and take notice of your breath and your body. Speak to yourself as you would a friend and resolve to try again.

INTENTIONS

Intentions are really interesting; they may feel like wishful thinking as you're putting pen to paper and figuring out what you're working toward, but this act of articulating what you want is a good way to develop your direction in life and toward your goals. If you struggle with "too many" ideas and goals, setting an intention may help clarify what is really important to you. Many of your disparate goals may have the same root intention!

When setting an intention, take it slow and listen to the voice inside your head. An intention is who you really are (without all those external influences) and is also a good reflection of who you want to be. Intentions should be positive and be a statement on how you want to be in the world. Try to begin with a "I" statement that backs up your goal.

SET YOUR GOALS BASED ON INTENTION

INTENTION

GOAL

GOAL

GOAL

THE BODY *achieves* WHAT THE MIND *believes*

HAPPY BODY, HAPPY MIND

EXERCISE IS NOT ONLY GOOD FOR YOUR PHYSICAL HEALTH, BUT FOR YOUR MENTAL HEALTH AND OVERALL WELLBEING TOO

We all know that exercise is good for us. Physical activity can help to improve your bone and muscle health, lower your risk of disease and injury, and improve life expectancy. But it's not only your body's health that will benefit; exercising improves our mental health and wellbeing too. It releases endorphins, which boost your mood and energy. Running for 15 minutes a day or walking for an hour can be as powerful as taking antidepressants. Moving more will help lower stress and anxiety levels, improve your sleep, sharpen your memory, and make you feel better about yourself.

A STEP AT A TIME

You don't need to worry about spending hours sweating at the gym or running a marathon as moderate amounts of exercise are just as beneficial. The aim is to do a manageable amount of activity on most days, so start off with a 15–30 minute walk and slowly increase the time.

OBSTACLES

If you're not used to exercising you might find it difficult to start, but five minutes a day is better than nothing. It's important not to get overwhelmed. If you're worried about other people, don't head straight to the gym. Try a gentle walk outside. Wear comfortable clothing, choose the time of day when you've got the most energy, and maybe ask a friend along so you don't start alone. Focus on fun activities that don't seem like exercise. Play catch with your kids in the yard, try out mini golf, or walk a nature trail. Just try moving more, whether it's cleaning the house or walking to the store instead of driving. Start out small and you'll soon notice the benefits.

BE A WARRIOR, NOT A WORRIER

YOGA IS NOT JUST A FORM OF EXERCISE; IT IS AN ANCIENT PRACTICE THAT BRINGS TOGETHER THE BODY AND MIND TO CREATE PERFECT HARMONY

When you think of yoga, you may think of people sitting cross-legged on mats saying "om," but practicing this form of exercise a few times a week is highly beneficial for both the body and the mind. The practice, which involves breathing, meditation, and different poses, focuses on strength, balance, and flexibility. Studies have shown it not only lowers stress and anxiety levels, but can also reduce inflammation, ease chronic pain, and improve heart health. It may also improve sleep quality and relieve migraines. Yoga can teach you mindfulness and, in turn, promote overall health.

GETTING STARTED

You don't have to go to the gym as there are plenty of videos on online to follow. You won't need much to start —just a yoga mat and comfortable clothing. Make sure you find a qualified teacher with whom you feel comfortable. It's important to know your limits, too. If you've just started you may not be as flexible as your instructor, so listen to your body. If you're doing a class with other people, don't compare yourself to others. Focus on yourself, remember to breathe, and remember to smile.

BE A POSER

The different poses in yoga include standing (such as mountain, downward dog, and warrior), balancing (such as tree pose), back bends (like cat/cow, bridge, cobra), seated (easy pose), and resting (child's pose). You don't have to start with a 45-minute class. Just practice 10–15 minutes of yoga to begin with and go from there. Even this will stretch your muscles and increase your range of motion.

MOUNTAIN

DOWNWARD DOG

WARRIOR I

TREE

BRIDGE

CAT

COW

COBRA

EASY POSE

CHILD'S POSE

THE WHOLE JOG

RUNNING IS A GREAT WAY TO RELIEVE STRESS AND GET HEALTHY, BUT HOW DO YOU GET STARTED?

STAY SAFE

Before you start running, check in with your doctor to make sure you are OK to run. Once you have the all clear, remember to warm up before you set off to avoid injuries. Take it easy. It's important to not go too fast at the beginning as you don't want to overexert yourself and then get frustrated and give up—or worse, hurt yourself.

BE PREPARED

Just like any other activity, you'll need to be prepared before starting. It's best to avoid food for one to two hours before exercise, but make sure you've eaten something—simple carbohydrates like a bagel with peanut butter will fuel your body. Ensure you have the right gear. A good pair of running shoes will prevent injuries, and sweat-wicking clothes will help you feel more comfortable. And finally, stay hydrated before, during, and after your run.

CURATE YOUR SENSES

If you find yourself counting down the minutes until your run is over, it might be worth curating your own music playlist to keep you motivated and to help the time fly by. Pick songs that make you want to get up and get moving, or even try a podcast to keep your brain occupied.

STEP BY STEP

You may want to get out there all guns blazing, but if you've never run before then you won't be ready for a marathon or a sprint. Start with short intervals—walk for two minutes and then jog for two minutes and so on. Each day you can increase the intervals by 30 seconds until you can run without stopping. Don't expect too much of yourself or you might lose your motivation.

WATCH YOUR FORM

It's important to make sure you have the right technique when running so that you don't injure yourself. Try to take short steps instead of long strides, don't hunch over, and position your chin so it isn't tilting up or downward. If you are aching in the wrong places, you may need to try running on a different surface as this can also have an effect on your body.

REST BETWEEN RUNS

If you're not a runner and you're just starting out, don't try to run every day. Ensure that you take a day to rest in between jogs to make sure your body has time to recover properly. If you are fit and want to exercise every day, try cross-training. Low-intensity exercises like swimming, cycling, or strength training will strengthen your muscles, bones, and heart without impacting your joints.

HIIT ME BABY ONE MORE TIME!

HIIT WORKOUTS AND WEIGHT TRAINING WILL NOT ONLY IMPROVE YOUR STRENGTH AND ENDURANCE, BUT ALSO THE GAINS YOU'LL RECEIVE FROM DOING THEM WILL BOOST YOUR CONFIDENCE AND HAVE YOU FEELING GREAT

MORE OXYGEN

High-Intensity Interval Training (HIIT) workouts are a fun way to get fit. While they're hard work, they are shorter than traditional exercise classes and they are very beneficial. HIIT involves short bursts of intense exercise followed by lower intensity periods. This makes you consume more oxygen, and not only gives you more energy during your workout, but can also improve your cardiovascular and overall health as well.

SIT UP STRAIGHT

Strength or resistance training involves using your own body weight or equipment, such as dumbbells or resistance bands, to build muscle, strength, and endurance. If you don't enjoy cardio, this is a great way to get in shape, but it also has other benefits. Strength training can help you improve your balance, give you better posture, increase your energy, improve your sleep, and even boost your mood.

A HEARTBEAT AWAY

Cardiovascular health is one of the most important physical benefits of exercise. After all, who doesn't want a healthy heart? Both HIIT workouts and strength training have been proven to be effective ways to significantly reduce blood pressure and heart rate without having to use medication. Strengthening your muscles can reduce hypertension and help lower the risk of heart disease. Just make sure you've had a health check-up before any exercise—if you have a heart condition, HIIT may not be suitable.

A BONE TO PICK

As we age we start to lose lean muscle mass. You may think the best exercises are high-intensity cardio, such as running, but weight training is just as important as it protects your bone health and muscle mass. Just 30 minutes of weight training will help increase bone density and reduce your risk of osteoporosis. Lifting weights will give you strength, power, and definition, and despite what some people think, you won't bulk out.

IT DOESN'T GET EASIER. YOU GET *stronger*

JUST KEEP BURNIN'

Both HIIT and strength training not only burn fat, but can also help you lose weight as your body continues to burn more calories after your workout. This is because, unlike cardio, these exercises increase your metabolic rate for hours after you exercise. Studies have shown that HIIT workouts burn 25–30 percent more fat than other forms of exercise in a shorter amount of time.

EXERCISE AND YOU

What form of exercise do you currently do?

How frequently do you currently exercise?

What exercise do you enjoy doing and why?

What exercise do you dislike and why?

What are you biggest obstacles when it comes to exercise?

WHAT IS YOUR LONG-TERM FITNESS GOAL?

Set some short-term fitness goals:

Why do you want to achieve your goals?

List everything that you need in order to achieve your fitness goals:

How will your measure progress?

FOOD, GLORIOUS FOOD

> FOOD HOLDS SO MUCH POWER FOR MANY OF US. IT'S OFTEN WHAT WE TURN TO ON A BAD DAY AND WE TEND TO CENTER CELEBRATIONS AROUND IT

Self-care isn't just a focus on your mental, spiritual, and emotional health; you also need to take care of your physical health, and food is a key component of this. What you put into your body fuels you and there are optimal ways to fuel your machine!

CHANGES

Nutrition is a science and there are levels that we should be working toward hitting in terms of vitamins and minerals. Start small and be kind to yourself; now is not the time to beat yourself up over a "bad" diet. Start by making small but important changes to your eating patterns. Drink one more glass of water than you would normally, avoid sugary foods, and don't skip breakfast! When we skip meals our blood sugar drops and you may feel more tired, irritable, and even depressed. Likewise, try not to let a small slip up affect your progress and your mood—we're all human and enjoying something "bad" isn't a sin. Try to reframe "bad" foods as "occasional" foods—nothing should be forbidden, otherwise you may be in danger of restricting your diet. Food should be a fun thing, so try something new and take stock of how this makes you feel.

BE GRATEFUL

Good physical health affects good mental health, and vice versa! When we feel good about our bodies, whether this is how they look or how they're working, we feel good about ourselves, and it really shows in your attitude to life.

A HEALTHY *outside* STARTS FROM THE *inside*

THE MOST IMPORTANT MEAL OF THE DAY

START YOUR DAY RIGHT WITH A BREAKFAST THAT WILL KEEP YOU FULL UNTIL LUNCHTIME! WHETHER YOU HAVE A SWEET OR SAVORY TOOTH, THERE ARE SO MANY CLEAN BREAKFASTS THAT YOU CAN WHIP UP FAST

GREEN SMOOTHIE

INGREDIENTS

- Unsweetened almond milk
- 1 banana
- 2 Tbsps frozen mango
- 2 Tbsps frozen peaches
- 1 tsp hemp hearts
- 1 tsp chia seeds
- 1 Tbsp peanut butter

Blend ingredients and top with a sprinkle of chia seeds.

EASY OMELET

INGREDIENTS

- 2 eggs
- 1 tsp butter

Crack eggs and whisk until mixed. Heat butter in pan and allow butter to foam. Add eggs and swirl around the pan until it is even, then cook on high until the eggs start to firm up. Add fillings of your choice. Fold one edge of the now-cooked eggs over and serve up.

OATMEAL

INGREDIENTS

- 1/2 cup (50g) steel-cut oats
- 1 1/2 cups (350mL) your choice of milk

Combine oats and milk in a saucepan and bring to a boil. Simmer for four minutes, remembering to stir! Try adding a healthy fat to your oatmeal to keep you full—nut butters or whole nuts/seeds help.

SHAKSHUKA

INGREDIENTS

- 1 can whole tomatoes
- 1 onion
- 1 tsp garlic
- 1 tsp coriander
- 1 tsp chili powder (add more for extra-hot)
- Olive oil

Soften garlic, herbs, and onions in a pan, add tomatoes, and cook until thickened. Make indentations in the sauce, then crack your eggs in. Put lid on pan and cook on low until the eggs are done.

OVERNIGHT OATS

INGREDIENTS

- 1/2 cup (50g) oats
- 1/2 cup (100mL) milk of your choice
- 1/2 cup (50g) berries
- 1 Tbsp peanut butter

Mix your oats with milk and refrigerate overnight. The next morning mix in your berries and peanut butter. If the oats are looking a bit thick, add some yogurt or an extra splash of milk.

MINDFUL EATING

HAVE YOU EVER FOUND YOURSELF CRAVING THROUGHOUT THE DAY, EATING BECAUSE YOU'RE BORED OR JUST BECAUSE YOU'RE FEELING "SNACKY"? TRY TO CONNECT WHAT YOU'RE EATING WITH MINDFUL EATING PRACTICES

Mindful eating is based on mindfulness meditation, helping you recognize what your body and emotions are really telling you. You work at being present in the moment, rather than being distracted or focusing on that next thing you need to do. It is all too easy to stop noticing how our bodies feel and we can end up living purely in our heads, which means that we end up disregarding the clues that our body is sending us!

WHY?

Mindful eating clues us in on the cues our body sends us and can help with cravings and any anxieties we may have around food. When we eat slowly and without distraction we can recognize more clearly when we're full—not just when we think we should be full. Mindful eating also helps us enjoy what we're eating. Remember, food isn't just fuel!

HOW?

A key part of mindfulness is reconnecting with our bodies and recognizing the sensations we experience. When we eat mindfully we should work at noticing the whole experience: the way the empty bowl feels in our hands, the temperature of the milk straight out of the fridge, not to mention the ranges of textures and tastes we experience every mealtime. Take a quiet moment next time you eat to practice mindful eating; take it slow, without distractions. If you find yourself becoming distracted, gently and kindly bring yourself back to the task at hand with a body scan; what is your body telling you about your mealtime?

FOOD POWER

FOOD HAS THE POWER TO MAKE YOU FEEL INCREDIBLE. FIND SOME SUPERFOODS BELOW TO HELP BOOST YOUR MOOD

OMEGA-3

Fat is often a dirty word when it comes to talking about healthy diets. However, we need healthy fats. It has been suggested that omega-3s may treat and prevent mood disorders. Omega-3 is also vital in cell manufacturing, keeping our hair and skin strong to ensure that we look like the happy people we are. Omega-3 fatty acids can be found in salmon, edamame beans, flax seeds, chia seeds, walnuts, and mackerel.

ENDORPHIN-ENCOURAGING FOODS.

Endorphins, one of your body's happy hormones, can be triggered by certain foods, such as dark chocolate, strawberries, oranges, and spicy foods. These foods can boost your mood as they stimulate your brain's production of endorphin levels. Higher endorphin levels are good as they enhance our immune system as well as our moods. If you reach for chocolate, go dark and stick with low sugar to avoid a crash.

STICK TO THE GOOD STUFF

A minimally processed diet is good for your mental and physical health. With the vast array of fad diets out there, it's hard to pick the one that is best for you. Keep it simple and follow a simple food guideline rather than a "diet"—eat more whole foods. Basically look for options that are minimally processed; the fewer "steps" the food has been though, the better.

MAGNESIUM

Magnesium plays a vital role in keeping our brains happy. Magnesium regulates our stress response system, controlling our levels of cortisol (a stress hormone). When we're low on magnesium we can feel more depressed, find it more difficult to get a good night's sleep, and can have trouble with our digestion. Magnesium can be found in dark-green leafy vegetables, legumes, nuts, and dark chocolate.

VITAMIN C

We all know how good vitamin C is for our immune system. When we feel run down we often feel depressed as well. Use this vitamin to combat both—a healthy body keeps a healthy mind too. Vitamin C also neutralizes free radicals, so you're eating to help protect your body. Vitamin C is found in an range of fruit and vegetables, such as peppers, broccoli, oranges, and blueberries.

VITAMIN D

Vitamin D helps fight off seasonal depression and helps regulate your mood. Serotonin is the key hormone that regulates our moods and is activated by vitamin D. Low levels of serotonin are linked to depression. Interestingly, vitamin D can be obtained from safe sun exposure, so if you live in a place with less sunshine then try to eat more salmon, mushrooms, eggs, and fortified milks.

BODY SCANS

When practicing any form of mindfulness meditation, a body scan is a helpful tool to understand what your body is telling you. Sit comfortably and notice the rhythm of your breath. Move your attention from the top of your head down your body gently, moving slowly but not sticking at any point. Observe any discomfort you may feel.

THINK ABOUT WHAT YOU ARE EATING

Eat your favorite food from childhood. What memories and feelings are conjured up when you are eating it? What is it that you really like about it? Do you still like it as much as you used to or have your tastes changed? How does that make you feel now.

MAKE A MEAL PLAN FOR NEXT WEEK

MONDAY	Breakfast	
	Lunch	
	Dinner	
	Snacks	
TUESDAY	Breakfast	
	Lunch	
	Dinner	
	Snacks	
WEDNESDAY	Breakfast	
	Lunch	
	Dinner	
	Snacks	

THURSDAY	Breakfast	
	Lunch	
	Dinner	
	Snacks	
FRIDAY	Breakfast	
	Lunch	
	Dinner	
	Snacks	
SATURDAY	Breakfast	
	Lunch	
	Dinner	
	Snacks	
SUNDAY	Breakfast	
	Lunch	
	Dinner	
	Snacks	

YOU GROW GIRL!

YOU MAY NOT REALIZE IT, BUT GETTING OUT IN NATURE CAN HAVE A POSITIVE IMPACT NOT ONLY ON YOUR PHYSICAL, BUT ALSO ON YOUR MENTAL HEALTH TOO

Have you ever wondered why you enjoy spending time walking through the park or sitting in your garden? Do you tend to feel happier when you're surrounded by nature? This is not just a coincidence. Research has shown that the environment we're in can have an effect on our physical and mental health. Being in nature can help reduce stress, lower blood pressure, reduce muscle tension, lower heart rate, and even extend your life. It can improve our mood and make us feel less anxious or sad. And we don't even have to be outside for it to have an impact. Indoor plants or even a picture of the outdoors can soothe us. One study showed that nature can go as far as helping hospital patients forget about the pain and discomfort they're feeling and heal faster. Another study showed nature can bring us together. People who shared a communal garden felt more connected to their community, spent more time with their neighbors, and even experienced lower levels of crime in the area. Those who spend more time outside, whether it's in their gardens, growing food in a community garden, exercising in a park, or going on a nature trail not only feel happier and more relaxed, but also are more active, have higher levels of self-esteem, and enjoy better health overall.

CATCHING THE SUN

Another reason to spend time outdoors is the sunshine. During the summer months, we get vitamin D from our exposure to direct sunlight. Our bodies need it as it helps absorb calcium and phosphate and ensures our bones stay healthy. During the winter months, when there's less direct sunlight, we need to get vitamin D from food sources, such as oily fish like salmon and mackerel, meat and eggs, or from supplements if needed.

NO
rain
NO
flowers

TAKE IT OUTSIDE

THERE ARE PLENTY OF WAYS TO GET IN TOUCH WITH NATURE, FROM YOUR DAILY EXERCISE TO FUN AND CREATIVE GREEN ACTIVITIES

A GOOD SEED FOR THE DAY

Gardening is a great way to improve your mental health. If you don't have a garden you could rent a plot in a community garden and grow vegetables, or you could even go fruit picking or foraging for the day. If you're more of a homebody, but don't have outdoor space, set up a window box to grow your own herbs.

MINDFUL MOVEMENT

All exercise is beneficial for your physical and mental health, but outdoor exercise is best. Whether it's a short stroll, playing a sport, swimming or cycling, move as much as you can while taking in the scenery and enjoying the fresh air. If you aren't a fitness fanatic why not try outdoor yoga to help you stretch and relax?

LET NATURE INSPIRE YOU

Green spaces are a great place to get creative. Sit outside and paint the landscape, make a picnic and eat it outdoors, or go stargazing. If you want to bring nature inside go on a woodland walk. You can take photos of the scenery to frame, or collect feathers, tree bark, and flowers to decorate your house.

CARING FOR THE ENVIRONMENT

If you're going to benefit from the environment, why not give something back in return? Instead of just going on a walk, you could go on a litter-picking walk. Rather than passively spending time in a green space, you could volunteer on a conservation project.

ANIMAL CONNECTIONS

Spending time in nature with animals is yet another fun way of being green. Whether you're birdwatching in your own garden, spotting squirrels as they scurry up trees in the park, hiking with your dog, or visiting a local farm, it is a great way to combat loneliness and give back to nature.

LET'S GO OUTSIDE

Take your journal to a green space. Sit outdoors and spend five minutes being mindful. Close your eyes. Listen to the sounds around you. What can you smell? Open your eyes and now think about what you can see. Feel the grass between your fingers. Now spend some time writing about what you experienced. How did it make you feel? Did it lift your mood? If you like to draw, why not do a sketch to describe your experience instead.

YOUR WRITING SPACE

YOUR DRAWING SPACE

FIND YOUR CENTER

KNOWN FOR HELPING PEOPLE FIND INNER PEACE AND HAPPINESS, THE ART OF MEDITATION CAN HELP YOU IN LOTS OF DIFFERENT ASPECTS OF YOUR LIFE

WHAT IS MEDITATION?

This ancient wellness practice is aimed at training your mind to focus and become more aware of yourself and your surroundings. By meditating we focus on being more mindful of what we are doing when we are doing it.

BECOME YOUR BEST SELF

Meditation can make you feel calm and relaxed, but it can do so much more than this. Studies have shown that practicing meditation can help reduce your levels of stress and anxiety and help you cope better with difficult situations. It can improve your mood and emotional health, help people battling depression, and develop your relationships with others. The benefits are not only physical—enhancing brain function, reducing blood pressure, and preventing heart disease—but mental too. Focusing on your mind and body can help you concentrate better for longer, boost memory, and even make you kinder and more compassionate. People who practice meditation tend to be more self-disciplined, more successful, and perform better in sports too. Studies have also shown that meditation can give you better quality of sleep, help you heal faster, make you more tolerant to pain, and even fight unwanted habits or addictions such as overeating. The positive effects are endless.

GETTING STARTED

You can meditate at any age or fitness level. It's easy to get started as you can practice anywhere and you don't need any equipment. There are lots of different styles of meditation so it's a good idea to try some guided exercises at first to find out which suits you best. Just a few minutes of daily meditation will make a big impact on your life so why not give it a go?

START THE DAY WITH MEDITATION

You can practice meditation at any time of day, but the ideal time is in the morning. Instead of waking up, checking your phone, and getting stressed looking at your to-do list, try meditating for five or ten minutes first. This will set the tone for the day. Instead of feeling overwhelmed, you'll feel calm and ready to tackle the tasks ahead. Meditation can clear your mind and give you more energy so you can be at your most productive.

WHAT'S YOUR MEDITATION STYLE?

THERE ARE HUNDREDS OF DIFFERENT MEDITATION TECHNIQUES, BUT THESE ARE JUST A FEW OF THE STYLES YOU COULD TRY TO SEE WHICH IS THE BEST FIT FOR YOU

MINDFULNESS MEDITATION

Mindfulness meditation is one of the most popular styles. The aim of this type of practice is to be mindful during your session by focusing your attention on your thoughts. Find somewhere quiet to sit for three to four minutes and free your mind. Concentrate on being present in the moment and be aware of what's going on in your head and body. If your thoughts start running away from you, concentrate on the positive and move away from the negative. Free yourself from judgment and open up your self-awareness. This can be done alone without a guide and you can even carry it out during your daily activities. Whether you're brushing your teeth, doing the dishes, or eating, use the time to focus on yourself. Mindfulness meditation can help reduce stress and depression by keeping you calm and relaxed.

VIPASSANA

Vipassana is one of the oldest Indian meditation techniques. The Buddhist term Vipassana means "seeing things clearly." It is all about learning to transform oneself through self-observation. While it can be practiced daily, it can take years to achieve liberation, which is the ultimate goal of this type of meditation. Vipassana involves focusing on a deeper connection between the mind and the body to understand the true nature of reality. It is a much more intense form of meditation as you contemplate some of the more difficult aspects of your existence from pain and suffering to emptiness and conflicts. You will concentrate on your physical sensations and examine your true self. Vipassana may help you see the world through new eyes. So much so that it has been used on prisoners to prevent them from re-offending.

HUMMING BEE PRANAYAMA

Humming bee pranayama meditation gets its name from the black Indian bee. The name refers to the sound you make while practicing this technique. It's practiced in a seated position. Sit with your eyes closed and focus on the sensations in your body. Place your fingers on the cartilage in the middle of each ear and gently press down as you breathe in and then, with your mouth closed, let out a high-pitched humming sound like a bee. Repeat this 3–4 times. The vibrations are believed to help calm you down almost instantly. This form of meditation is used to help you rid your body of anger. You can also try this lying down or lying on your right side. Humming bee pranayama has proven helpful in reducing blood pressure and headaches in particular.

MANTRA

Manta meditation comes from the word "man," which means mind, and the word "tra," which means release. This ancient Hindu and Buddhist practice involves repeating a sound, word, or phrase to help clear your mind. Many practitioners use the word "om," while others prefer to repeat affirmations such as "shanti," which means peace, to help guide their thoughts to a positive space. The sound can be spoken loudly or quietly—whichever works best for you. The repetitiveness keeps you alert and helps you stay in tune, not only with yourself, but also with your surroundings. It gives you a deeper level of awareness. You may enjoy this style of meditation more because it is easier to focus on a word than on your breath. If you're having difficulties focusing, don't fret. Just keep practicing. This will help you get in the right frame of mind.

ZAZEN MEDITATION

The Japanese word Zazen translates as "seated meditation." This form of meditation originates from Zen Buddhism in China. Practitioners usually sit in a lotus or half-lotus position with their legs crossed and their back straight for this technique. Zen means concentration or meditation. The aim is to concentrate on your breath, posture, and thought process so that you can eventually clear your mind completely and find spiritual awakenment. Unlike in mindfulness meditation, where you focus on a specific object, zen meditation seeks general awareness. Observe the world around you and free your mind of thoughts and emotions. This type of meditation is often practiced with your eyes semi-open for this purpose. Focus on your breath as it moves from your belly and on being quietly self-aware. Think about nothing and eventually you will feel completely at peace.

TAI CHI

Tai chi is an ancient Chinese tradition, which involves gentle flowing movements and stretches. It was originally developed as a form of self-defense, but it has gradually evolved into graceful exercises. It is also used as a form of meditation as, while you move, your focus is on slow, deep breathing. As you move, you flow from one posture to the next without stopping. The practice is often referred to as meditation in motion. No equipment is needed for this type of meditation, but you should try to practice it somewhere that will allow you to feel calm. This could be in a quiet space of your house or in a park. Anyone can do tai chi as the exercises are low impact. As you move, you will not only strengthen your muscles and balance, but you will also improve your mood and energy. There is evidence that practicing tai chi can reduce your stress levels.

YOGA NIDRA

While many types of meditation are done in a seated position, yoga nidra is practiced lying down. Also known as "yogic sleep" or "effortless relaxation," this type of meditation is for people who have trouble letting go. The aim of yoga nidra is to find yourself in between the state of sleep and awareness. Lie down, close your eyes, relax your body completely, and look inward. Let your instructor help you become aware of your inner world. You will feel completely restored by the end of the practice. Again, no equipment is needed; however, some people choose to use pillows and blankets to make themselves more comfortable. Yoga nidra will not only help improve the quality of your sleep, but it'll teach you to be still and let go of tension and pain so that you can connect with yourself and enjoy life to the fullest.

QUIET THE *mind* AND THE *soul* WILL SPEAK

KINHIN

Kinhin meditation is a type of walking meditation. Here you walk between two long periods of sitting meditation. The benefit of this type is that, because you are walking, you can practice it for longer. The aim is to move while staying focused on your meditation. Start by walking round the room in a clockwise direction with your hands clasped together in shahsu (your left hand in a fist with your right hand over it). Concentrate on your posture and as you walk, bring the rhythm of your movement together with the rhythm of your breath. As your foot takes a step down on to the ground, breathe out, and then as your body relaxes, breathe in and take another step forward. Repeat this sequence for about 10 minutes. Make sure your hands are in a comfortable position, that you are aware of balancing the movement of your body and focusing on the energy in your feet.

FIND YOUR MANTRA

Mantra is good practice for morning meditation. Write down five mantras for the day ahead. For example: "I am resilient." Then close your eyes and repeat each mantra several times while focusing on your breath, being aware of yourself and your mantra.

ONE

TWO

THREE

FOUR

FIVE

I AM *enough*

THE MORE *grateful* I AM, THE MORE *beauty* I SEE

GET PRACTICING

GRATITUDE DOESN'T NEED TO BE RESERVED FOR MASSIVE EVENTS; YOU CAN PRACTICE GRATITUDE FOR THE LITTLE THINGS IN LIFE TO INVITE MORE JOY

WHAT IT IS

Gratitude journaling is, in short, the practice of writing down the things you are grateful for, whether big or small. Gratitude is an important emotion to experience as it helps us to become more positive and emotionally balanced. Writing these emotions down is important to log them in your head as well as to give us something to look back on in our less positive moments. Gratitude journaling may seem like a soft skill to learn, but it has an enormous effect on your wellbeing.

BENEFITS

There are great benefits in saying "thank you." The simple act of writing down the things you are thankful for has amazing benefits for your mental health. By spilling your brain onto paper you may find that you sleep better, have fewer symptoms of illness, and feel happier overall. Writing helps to organize your thoughts and may help you to unconsciously solve problems and difficulties in your life. You may very well find it has an effect on your dreams, too. You're also rewiring your brain to think positively. When thinking about the people we feel grateful for (and their actions), we're also practicing empathy for others, which can only be a good thing! Practicing gratitude for people and events in our lives can also help make us less materialistic; we recognize that there is more value in the simple things in life rather than acquiring the newest gadget or flashiest car.

OVERFLOW

It is important to allow gratitude to spill into your everyday life. There is no benefit in being grateful and positive every night in your journal but expecting the worst every time you step out of your front door. When you start looking for things to be grateful for, you will find there is more to feel positive about. In terms of positive thinking, like attracts like.

HELPFUL HINTS

A BLANK PAGE IS OFTEN THE MOST TERRIFYING THING WHEN BEGINNING A JOURNAL, SO TAKE A LOOK AT THE FOLLOWING TIPS TO HELP YOU MAKE THAT FIRST MARK ON PAPER

NOTICE NEW THINGS

Try to adjust what you're thankful and grateful for every time you journal. Drill down and go into detail as to what it is that you're specifically grateful for, whether this is the way your dog greets you every morning or the specific method that helps you make a great cup of tea.

SURPRISING STUFF

You may find yourself feeling more strongly when practicing and recording gratitude for surprising events. A reaction to something unexpected is a strong emotion, and you're essentially rewiring what your brain is experiencing. Often the intensity of emotion is directly linked to how much you're expecting it!

ENJOYING LIFE IS THE GREATEST ART

WHO RATHER THAN WHAT

When journaling gratitude try to turn your entries on their head by focusing on the "who" rather than the "what." We should always try to focus on the action and intention behind the things we are grateful for rather than the thing itself.

WORK CONSCIOUSLY

Instead of working by rote and feeling like gratitude journaling is something on your "must-do" list, try to make the conscious decision of focusing on your motivation for journaling. Open yourself up to the positives in life as you reflect on the good that has come your way.

MAKE IT A HABIT

It is far better to do a little journaling every day, or every few days, than one big session. Practicing gratitude is a skill and one that you should practice regularly to exercise and strengthen that part of your brain, let alone using the activity to invite more good things into your life!

I AM GRATEFUL

USE THESE PAGES TO REALLY THINK ABOUT WHAT YOU ARE GRATEFUL FOR IN LIFE. I AM GRATEFUL FOR MY . . .

FAMILY BECAUSE . . .

FRIENDS BECAUSE . . .

CAREER BECAUSE . . .

BODY BECAUSE . . .

PAST BECAUSE . . .

ABILITIES TO . . .

ACCESS TO . . .

LOVE OF . . .

EDUCATION BECAUSE . . .

PURPOSEFUL PASTIMES

FROM READING AND SWIMMING TO COLLECTING STAMPS OR PLAYING CHESS, OUR FAVORITE HOBBIES ARE NOT ONLY FUN, BUT THEY'RE ALSO GOOD FOR US, WHICH MAKES THEM A WINNING COMBINATION

YOU TIME

Our hobbies give us time for ourselves. Whether we're reading alone or playing a sport with other people, it gives us a chance to enjoy doing something we love. This is not only beneficial for our state of mind, but also our physical health too. Creative hobbies like drawing, baking, or knitting, engaging your brain by doing a puzzle, learning a new language, or moving your body by swimming or playing football, all help improve your quality of life.

STRESS LESS

Studies show that having hobbies can help reduce levels of stress by 34 percent and sadness by 18 percent. This is simply because, if we make time for ourselves, we feel less stressed and more happy. Focusing on a fun task can help us relax and be more present as we enjoy the moment. If you have activities that you can look forward to it makes the difficult things in life seem a little easier or at least more bearable.

BRAIN POWER

When we spend time on our hobbies we use our brain cells, whether it's figuring out how to build a model airplane or devising a strategy for winning a hockey game. This not only boosts our cognitive function, but also it makes us more alert and helps us focus more. It can even improve our confidence as, generally, we tend to be better at activities we enjoy.

CONNECTIONS

Doing what we love can also help us meet new people who are passionate about the same things. There are few things more beneficial than joining a community. By making new connections we improve our wellbeing, as bonding with others is good for our health.

LET'S DO WHAT WE

love

AND DO A LOT OF IT

5 HELPFUL HOBBIES

ALL HOBBIES ARE VALID, BUT SOME CAN REALLY BOOST YOUR WELLBEING BY IMPROVING YOUR PHYSICAL AND MENTAL HEALTH, COORDINATION, KNOWLEDGE, OR STAMINA

PLAY MIND GAMES

Games such as chess or sudoku are a fun way of improving our cognitive functions. Chess helps us use both sides of our brains (the side that recognizes objects and the side that recognizes patterns). It can also help us improve our memory and strategic thinking.

CURL UP WITH A GOOD BOOK

Reading and writing are not only good ways of spending time by yourself, but they can give you a creative outlet, which is good for your mind. If you're having a bad day you can escape your worries by writing your own story or letting a book transport you to a different world.

HAVE A BALL

Team sports such as baseball or basketball are not only fun, but they're a good form of exercise, so great for your physical health. They are also a way of being social, and offer team building and strategic thinking, which are all positive benefits for your mental health.

MAKE IT SPECIAL

Specialist subjects like collecting stamps or astrology are a good way to relax, instead of being glued to a screen, but they are also beneficial for your mental wellbeing. Stamp collecting can help you develop patience and focus more. Astrology can improve your self-awareness as you study your character, recognize your potential and grow spiritually.

LEARN THE ART OF SELF-DEFENSE

Martial arts, such as karate, can improve your balance, stamina, and coordination, as well as teaching you about self-discipline. They are not only great for your physical health, building strength and flexibility, but they are also known to help you feel less stressed and anxious. This is because the exercises focus on breathing and control.

WHAT ARE YOUR FAVORITE HOBBIES?

Write down five of your favorite pastimes. Then write down the mental and physical benefits of each of them. This will help you to learn to appreciate them.

HOBBY ONE

HOBBY TWO

HOBBY THREE

HOBBY FOUR

HOBBY FIVE

THE WORST ENEMY OF *creativity* IS SELF-DOUBT

GET CREATIVE

> ART CAN HAVE A CALMING EFFECT ON A PERSON; YOU CAN SPEND TIME FOCUSING ON ONE TASK, BEING FULLY IN THE MOMENT. ART CAN ALSO GIVE US GREAT JOY

Many psychologists believe that making art is as important as food, exercise, and meditation due to the positive effects it has on our mental and physical health. While we may not regard it as highly as nutrition or other basic human needs, exercising our creative muscles is a key part of human wellness.

WHY IS CREATIVITY IMPORTANT?

Being creative is a great way to keep our minds open and active. We're constantly learning news things in life, but sometimes you can get stuck in one way of thinking, which is detrimental to your overall wellness. By trying something new or unexpected in the name of art and creativity, we engage different learning styles. In adopting more patterns of wellness we're breaking out of the every day autopilot routines, and nowhere can you do that more easily than in art! Interestingly, research has found that creativity supports our health—it creates and strengthens our neural networks in our brain. Your quality of life is also improved if you surround yourself with things that you enjoy, value, and find beautiful.

HOW CAN YOU BE CREATIVE?

There are so many ways to tap into our creative impulses; getting creative doesn't have to be an expensive hobby either!

If you don't have the "right" materials work with what you have—cotton buds and scrunched up tissue make amazing marks with paint and inks. Many hobby stores sell test kits for you to dip into a new creative hobby inexpensively—try something you'd never consider, you may find a new passion!

MAKE A MARK

WHILE YOU MAY NOT FEEL LIKE THE "ARTY TYPE," IT'S IMPORTANT TO TREAT YOURSELF AS YOU WOULD A FRIEND AND ENCOURAGE EXPERIMENTATION IN YOUR CREATIVE PURSUITS—PAINTING DOESN'T HAVE TO BE SCARY!

PAINT BY NUMBERS

Adult paint-by-number kits are growing in popularity as a way to get in the creative zone and meditate a bit. As you are presented with the "right" colors and the outlines are done for you, there is no worry about proportion or composition!

COLOR THEORY

Play with colors. While we have been taught about primary and secondary colors, we may have forgotten the lessons on how these colors interact. Try unusual color combinations; do these trigger memories or associations in you? Give color mixing a try. Lean in to the "what if I . . ."

GET MESSY

Engaging in the visual arts is a great way to express yourself creatively. Now this doesn't have to be in the form of an organized class or even around other people, if you're feeling shy about your skills. Painting is an excellent way to practice mindful action; we're literally creating something out of nothing! Enjoy the action of mixing paint and don't focus too hard on the end goal. You may find that as you play (and art should be play!) you uncover how you're feeling about whatever is on your mind. Many artists say paint does not lie.

KILL PERFECTIONISM

So many of us enjoyed art as children, only to be caught up in "not being good enough" as we grew. Nix that pattern of thought. All art is good art, even the "bad" stuff! Acknowledge your feelings but remember you aren't creating for anyone else but you.

STILL LIFE

Still lifes are a classic subject for art all over the world for good reason! Collect a group of objects from around your house and arrange them interestingly; try quick thumbnail (small) sketches to decide on your arrangement.

DEVELOP YOUR STYLE

Take a moment to think about what kind of an artist you are; do you have patience to accurately capture detail, or are you more interested in light, color, and feeling in paint? Think about what it is that inspires you about your favorite artists.

CREATE WITH YOUR HANDS

BE OPEN TO TRYING NEW THINGS; THIS ARTISTIC CREATIVITY CAN FOLLOW YOU THROUGH TO OTHER AREAS OF YOUR LIFE. PICK UP A NEW CREATIVE PROJECT FROM THE LIST BELOW

KNITTING

Knitting has many health benefits (both mental and physical). Knitting inspires a feeling of "flow": that moment when you are in the zone and time doesn't matter any more. Knitting is great as you are also physically constructing an item. Interestingly, repetitive motions like knitting trigger serotonin release (our calm chemical).

You don't have to start with a complicated project. Something as simple as a scarf will be a good start. Enjoy the process and be mindful of what senses you are activating.

POSTCARDS

Blank packs of postcards can be bought at many stationery, art, and newsstands. Decorate the fronts in anyway you wish; pencils, paint, or pastels (use hairspray to "set" that last one) and send them by snail mail to your loved ones. Postcards are a great medium as they're not too big or small! Not only are you being creative, you're also showing your appreciation for those you send the postcards to; you show they are in your thoughts.

COLLAGE

So many of us have stacks of old magazines around the house. Why not take the opportunity to clear some clutter and get creative with some collage! You can use text to create a collage poem, or an inspiration and intention board to solidify your goals. Search for positive words or fonts and designs you like—put them together to inspire you. Browse through for relaxing images and cut and stick to your heart's content.

BAKING

You can find meditative practices in kneading bread, icing cakes, and making cookies—in a way you're grounding yourself to your present moment. Baking is different to many of the other creative hobbies on this list as it also takes in the taste sense (something we don't recommend with paint!). While baking is a science to an extent, it also allows a massive amount of creative freedom with flavor combinations. Try to practice gratitude while baking, and think about where your ingredients came from.

CLAY

Clay is one of the most tactile materials to be creative with, mindfully. Our fingertips are full of nerve endings and playing with air-drying clay can have amazing therapeutic benefits as you're connecting your body with what you're seeing. You don't need a pottery wheel to create; experiment with pinch pots, coil pots, and slab pots (think about making a cube with your clay). Polymer clay is also easy to work with and can result in amazing jewelry creations.

MAKE SOME NOISE

We are all naturally creative. Making art may not be your forte, but music, dance, and singing are also integral to our wellness and wellbeing and are easily accessible to all. So even if you haven't picked up a musical instrument since school you can still feel the benefit from learning to play music. If you're feeling shy, try singing in the shower—the acoustics are great and singing a favorite tune will be sure to put you in a great mood.

Musical training can develop positive changes in our brains, mainly between the two hemispheres! Remember to be kind in our expectations of ourselves; you simply cannot become a musical prodigy overnight. Use a kind inner voice when learning a new skill. Take a moment to think what you want out of this new creative hobby; are you making up for something you didn't get as a child or is there a specific piece of music you want to master? These answers will point you to the heart of your musical creativity.

ZENTANGLE DRAWING

Zentangle drawing is a relaxing way to create beautiful images by drawing unplanned, but structured patterns. Draw random patterns to allow your brain to enter a state of slow. Make patterns with dots, dashes, strings, squares, etc. Let your hand draw freely . . .

GIVING BACK

HELPING OTHERS MAY NOT CHANGE THE WHOLE WORLD, BUT IT COULD CHANGE IT FOR ONE PERSON, AND YOU NEVER KNOW HOW IT MIGHT HELP YOU TOO

Helping others is much more than just doing a good deed. You'll be doing a world of good, not only for the person you're helping, but also for yourself and others.

HEALTH

Research has shown that helping people can not only lower your blood pressure, but it can also reduce stress and loneliness, relieve symptoms of chronic pain, and make you live longer. Many people have found that focusing on others takes your attention away from the stresses on your own body, improves your mood, and boosts your overall health and wellbeing.

PASS IT ON

The best aspect of giving back is that it is contagious. The more you help others, the more people will want to do the same and kindness will spread.

HAPPINESS

Whether it's volunteering at a hospital, helping a friend with a problem, or simply asking a colleague how they are, kindness goes a long way. When we do something kind without feeling like it is a duty, we feel better about ourselves and it makes us kinder, more empathetic, and more supportive. Giving back can give us a sense of purpose knowing we've done something of value and it can help us make connections as we build friendships.

KINDNESS IS A GIFT EVERYONE CAN AFFORD TO GIVE

HELP YOURSELF

Helping others can also help you. Mentoring a schoolchild may give you a sense of accomplishment and watching them grow may help you with your self-esteem. Volunteering at a soup kitchen or homeless shelter can change your perspective on life those around you. People who give back to their local communities often come away with a glass-half-full approach to life.

KINDNESS MATTERS

A KIND ACT GOES A LONG WAY. HERE ARE JUST FIVE WAYS YOU CAN HELP OTHERS AND GET BACK AS MUCH AS YOU GIVE

DONATE

Whether you're donating your time by volunteering at a soup kitchen or on a natural relief campaign, donating toys to an orphanage, canned goods to a food bank, or clothes to charity, you'll not only be helping those less fortunate than you, but you'll be a better person for it.

ADOPT

Adopting a rescue animal or even a child is a huge contribution to society. You'll not only be giving them a roof over their head, a place to sleep, and food to eat, but also you'll be showing them love, which you'll receive in return, so it's a win-win situation.

DONATE MORE

It's not just time and goods you can donate. Why not sign up to become a blood or organ donor and help save a life on another level? Giving blood doesn't take long and it's always in short supply. By becoming an organ donor, your organs could help someone else live, making a huge impact with one kind gesture.

HELP YOUR COMMUNITY

There are so many ways to give back to your community from volunteering at a retirement home to becoming a volunteer firefighter. Mentor schoolchildren, become a scout or brownie leader, or coach a sports team. If you're not a people person, go to a litter-picking event, help out at a community garden, or be a fundraiser.

GIVING IS THE GREATEST ACT OF GRACE

HELP YOUR NEIGHBORS

Giving back doesn't have to be a huge job or take up a whole day. You can start small by helping a friend or neighbor with mowing the lawn or DIY jobs if they're struggling. Help someone elderly cross the road or carry a stroller for a parent who needs help.

RANDOM ACTS OF KINDNESS

Spend some time thinking about kind gestures that you could do for other people—both strangers and people you know. It could be as simple as paying for a coffee for the person next to you in line at the coffee shop, leaving flowers on a doorstep, or doing something that you know will really help someone. Could you go to the supermarket for an elderly neighbor or take them some homemade cakes?

Random act of kindness ....

Day complete ....

How did it make you feel? ....

....

Random act of kindness ....

Day complete ....

How did it make you feel? ....

....

Random act of kindness ....

Day complete ....

How did it make you feel? ....

....

Random act of kindness ....

Day complete ....

How did it make you feel? ....

....

Random act of kindness ....

Day complete ....

How did it make you feel? ....

....

Random act of kindness ....

Day complete ....

How did it make you feel? ....

....

Random act of kindness ....

Day complete ....

How did it make you feel? ....

....

Random act of kindness ....

Day complete ....

How did it make you feel? ....

....

SLEEP TIGHT

SLEEP NOT ONLY MAINTAINS OUR BODIES, BUT IT ALSO ALLOWS OUR BRAINS TO PROCESS INFORMATION. WHILE SO MUCH OF SLEEP IS STILL A MYSTERY TO SCIENTISTS, WE ALL KNOW HOW VALUABLE IT IS WHEN WE MISS OUT ON IT!

Sleep is just as important as diet and exercise for our overall wellness, and it can appear to be easy to get under control—after all we do it "in our sleep." But so many of us suffer from either poor quality sleep or a small quantity of it! It is important to keep in mind that we are all different and you may require more or less sleep than a friend or partner.

If you're having sleep issues, try to approach these problems mindfully without too much judgment. Stressing about a lack of sleep will only put you in a thought cycle. Try to acknowledge what you're feeling.

WHAT HAPPENS WHEN WE SLEEP?

When you sleep, your body clock takes over; you may have heard of a circadian rhythm, which increases the drive to go to sleep. Your body clock is affected by light and darkness as well as any other cues you have "trained" your body to look for as a sign that sleep is near. When evening comes your body releases melatonin (the hormone that makes you feel sleepy) and cortisol is released when the sun rises. There are so many things that can disrupt our natural rhythms: TV screens, smartphones, and sugar, for example.

SLEEP AND OUR HEALTH

Poor sleep, or not enough of it, has strong links to poor mental and physical health. In short, sleep helps your brain and your body work. You're preparing for whatever life throws at you the next day.

Sleep deficiency alters our brains; we may have trouble controlling our emotions, lack motivation, and feel stress more readily. Frustratingly, people who lack good sleep often feel depressed, and people who are depressed often don't get good sleep—we need to work toward breaking this cycle.

SLEEP IS THE BEST *meditation*

IMPROVE YOUR SLEEP SPACE

THE AVERAGE PERSON SPENDS AROUND 33 YEARS OF THEIR LIFE IN BED! QUALITY SLEEP HELPS YOU STAY ALERT AND FOCUSED DURING THE DAY AND CAN HELP WITH WEIGHT MANAGEMENT AND GOOD MENTAL HEALTH. MAKE YOUR BEDROOM THE BEST IT CAN BE

FRESHEN YOUR PILLOW

Take a moment to think about when you bought your pillow. So many of us are sleeping on old pillows that provide no neck support. Whether you're a side, back, or front sleeper there is an optimum pillow for you out there. Treat yourself and see how much your sleep improves.

COOL IT DOWN

There's nothing like getting cozy before bed, but did you know that overheating is a main cause for waking in the night as your core temperature needs to drop for you to fall (and stay) asleep? If you live in a hot climate this may be tricky, but a fan can help (and provide white noise at the same time).

LET'S GET DARK

It's no secret that light wakes us up, so when you're looking to sleep, irritating lights are the last thing you need! If you need to reset your sleep cycle, eliminate light! Invest in heavy curtains (that double up as noise blockers) and try not to use bright lights in your room before sleep.

TIDY UP

Clutter around the house can cause stress and this is doubly true in a bedroom; you don't need to see a visual reminder of all your "didn't dos" before you drift off! Take a moment and clear the clutter, pick up laundry from the floor, clear your bedside table, and commit to keeping things neat.

TURN OFF THE TECH

Try to stop using your blue-light-producing devices around 30 minutes before bed. Blue light from smartphones restrains the production of melatonin (the hormone that controls your sleep cycle). It's also super easy to get anxious or angry about something you read or interact with. Help your brain turn off and hide your phone!

LET'S MONITOR YOUR SLEEP

MONDAY

How many hours of sleep did you get? ....

Describe the quality of your sleep ....

....

Did you have dreams or nightmares? ....

What did you do before bed? ....

....

TUESDAY

How many hours of sleep did you get? ....

Describe the quality of your sleep ....

....

Did you have dreams or nightmares? ....

What did you do before bed? ....

....

WEDNESDAY

How many hours of sleep did you get? ....

Describe the quality of your sleep ....

....

Did you have dreams or nightmares? ....

What did you do before bed? ....

....

THURSDAY

How many hours of sleep did you get? ....

Describe the quality of your sleep ....

....

Did you have dreams or nightmares? ....

What did you do before bed? ....

....

FRIDAY

How many hours of sleep did you get? ....

Describe the quality of your sleep ....

....

Did you have dreams or nightmares? ....

What did you do before bed? ....

....

SATURDAY

How many hours of sleep did you get? ....

Describe the quality of your sleep ....

....

Did you have dreams or nightmares? ....

What did you do before bed? ....

....

SUNDAY

How many hours of sleep did you get? ....

Describe the quality of your sleep ....

....

Did you have dreams or nightmares? ....

What did you do before bed? ....

....

66 days OF SELF-CARE JOURNALING

MAKE YOUR WELLBEING THE MOST IMPORTANT PART OF YOUR DAY. THIS WILL HELP YOU TO CREATE A MINDFUL AND POSITIVE ROUTINE IN ORDER TO TAKE CARE OF YOURSELF

The main goal of this *Self-Care Journal* is to encourage you to think about your wellbeing every single day. So, we're going to set you a challenge. The following section is split into 66 days. On each day, record your sleep, daily activities, and what you have eaten. You'll also be prompted to think about the positive parts of your day as well as an opportunity to practice gratitude. Your challenge is to keep this up for 66 consecutive days and create a positive habit that will help to nurture you.

DAY 1

My intentions for the day are . . .

Sleep quality:

Today's activities will be:

Hours of sleep:

Today I ate . . .

My self-care plan for the day includes . . .

The best part of today was . . .

Today I am grateful for . . .

Mood tracker

DAY 2

My intentions for the day are . . .

Sleep quality:

Hours of sleep:

Today I ate . . .

Today's activities will be:

My self-care plan for the day includes . . .

The best part of today was . . .

Today I am grateful for . . .

Mood tracker

DAY 3

My intentions for the day are . . .

Sleep quality:

Hours of sleep:

Today I ate . . .

Today's activities will be:

My self-care plan for the day includes . . .

The best part of today was . . .

Today I am grateful for . . .

Mood tracker

DAY 4

My intentions for the day are . . .

Sleep quality:

Hours of sleep:

Today I ate . . .

Today's activities will be:

My self-care plan for the day includes . . .

The best part of today was . . .

Today I am grateful for . . .

Mood tracker

DAY 5

My intentions for the day are . . .

Sleep quality:

Hours of sleep:

Today I ate . . .

Today's activities will be:

My self-care plan for the day includes . . .

The best part of today was . . .

Today I am grateful for . . .

Mood tracker

DAY 6

My intentions for the day are . . .

Sleep quality:

Hours of sleep:

Today I ate . . .

Today's activities will be:

My self-care plan for the day includes . . .

The best part of today was . . .

Today I am grateful for . . .

Mood tracker

DAY 7

My intentions for the day are . . .

Sleep quality:

Hours of sleep:

Today I ate . . .

Today's activities will be:

My self-care plan for the day includes . . .

The best part of today was . . .

Today I am grateful for . . .

Mood tracker

DAY 8

My intentions for the day are . . .

Sleep quality:

Today's activities will be:

Hours of sleep:

Today I ate . . .

My self-care plan for the day includes . . .

The best part of today was . . .

Today I am grateful for . . .

Mood tracker

DAY 9

My intentions for the day are . . .

Sleep quality:

Today's activities will be:

Hours of sleep:

Today I ate . . .

My self-care plan for the day includes . . .

The best part of today was . . .

Today I am grateful for . . .

Mood tracker

DAY 10

My intentions for the day are . . .

Sleep quality:

Hours of sleep:

Today I ate . . .

Today's activities will be:

My self-care plan for the day includes . . .

The best part of today was . . .

Today I am grateful for . . .

Mood tracker

DAY 11

My intentions for the day are . . .

Sleep quality:

Hours of sleep:

Today I ate . . .

Today's activities will be:

My self-care plan for the day includes . . .

The best part of today was . . .

Today I am grateful for . . .

Mood tracker

DAY 12

My intentions for the day are . . .

Sleep quality:

Today's activities will be:

Hours of sleep:

Today I ate . . .

My self-care plan for the day includes . . .

The best part of today was . . .

Today I am grateful for . . .

Mood tracker

DAY 13

My intentions for the day are . . .

Sleep quality:

Hours of sleep:

Today I ate . . .

Today's activities will be:

My self-care plan for the day includes . . .

The best part of today was . . .

Today I am grateful for . . .

Mood tracker

DAY 14

My intentions for the day are . . .

Sleep quality:

Hours of sleep:

Today's activities will be:

Today I ate . . .

My self-care plan for the day includes . . .

The best part of today was . . .

Today I am grateful for . . .

Mood tracker

DAY 15

My intentions for the day are . . .

Sleep quality:

Hours of sleep:

Today's activities will be:

Today I ate . . .

My self-care plan for the day includes . . .

The best part of today was . . .

Today I am grateful for . . .

Mood tracker

DAY 16

My intentions for the day are . . .

Sleep quality:

Hours of sleep:

Today's activities will be:

Today I ate . . .

My self-care plan for the day includes . . .

The best part of today was . . .

Today I am grateful for . . .

Mood tracker

DAY 17

My intentions for the day are . . .

Sleep quality:

Hours of sleep:

Today I ate . . .

Today's activities will be:

My self-care plan for the day includes . . .

The best part of today was . . .

Today I am grateful for . . .

Mood tracker

DAY 18

My intentions for the day are . . .

Sleep quality:

Hours of sleep:

Today's activities will be:

Today I ate . . .

My self-care plan for the day includes . . .

The best part of today was . . .

Today I am grateful for . . .

Mood tracker

DAY 19

My intentions for the day are . . .

Sleep quality:

Hours of sleep:

Today I ate . . .

Today's activities will be:

My self-care plan for the day includes . . .

The best part of today was . . .

Today I am grateful for . . .

Mood tracker

DAY 20

My intentions for the day are . . .

Sleep quality:

Hours of sleep:

Today I ate . . .

Today's activities will be:

My self-care plan for the day includes . . .

The best part of today was . . .

Today I am grateful for . . .

Mood tracker

DAY 21

My intentions for the day are . . .

Sleep quality:

Hours of sleep:

Today I ate . . .

Today's activities will be:

My self-care plan for the day includes . . .

The best part of today was . . .

Today I am grateful for . . .

Mood tracker

DAY 22

My intentions for the day are . . .

Sleep quality:

Hours of sleep:

Today I ate . . .

Today's activities will be:

My self-care plan for the day includes . . .

The best part of today was . . .

Today I am grateful for . . .

Mood tracker

DAY 23

My intentions for the day are . . .

Sleep quality:

Hours of sleep:

Today I ate . . .

Today's activities will be:

My self-care plan for the day includes . . .

The best part of today was . . .

Today I am grateful for . . .

Mood tracker

DAY 24

My intentions for the day are . . .

Sleep quality:

Hours of sleep:

Today's activities will be:

Today I ate . . .

My self-care plan for the day includes . . .

The best part of today was . . .

Today I am grateful for . . .

Mood tracker

DAY 25

My intentions for the day are . . .

Sleep quality:

Hours of sleep:

Today I ate . . .

Today's activities will be:

My self-care plan for the day includes . . .

The best part of today was . . .

Today I am grateful for . . .

Mood tracker

DAY 26

My intentions for the day are . . .

Sleep quality:

Today's activities will be:

Hours of sleep:

Today I ate . . .

My self-care plan for the day includes . . .

The best part of today was . . .

Today I am grateful for . . .

Mood tracker

DAY 27

My intentions for the day are . . .

Sleep quality:

Hours of sleep:

Today I ate . . .

Today's activities will be:

My self-care plan for the day includes . . .

The best part of today was . . .

Today I am grateful for . . .

Mood tracker

DAY 28

My intentions for the day are . . .

Sleep quality:

Hours of sleep:

Today I ate . . .

Today's activities will be:

My self-care plan for the day includes . . .

The best part of today was . . .

Today I am grateful for . . .

Mood tracker

DAY 29

My intentions for the day are . . .

Sleep quality:

Today's activities will be:

Hours of sleep:

Today I ate . . .

My self-care plan for the day includes . . .

The best part of today was . . .

Today I am grateful for . . .

Mood tracker

DAY 30

My intentions for the day are . . .

Sleep quality:

Today's activities will be:

Hours of sleep:

Today I ate . . .

My self-care plan for the day includes . . .

The best part of today was . . .

Today I am grateful for . . .

Mood tracker

DAY 31

My intentions for the day are . . .

Sleep quality:

Today's activities will be:

Hours of sleep:

Today I ate . . .

My self-care plan for the day includes . . .

The best part of today was . . .

Today I am grateful for . . .

Mood tracker

DAY 32

My intentions for the day are . . .

Sleep quality:

Hours of sleep:

Today's activities will be:

Today I ate . . .

My self-care plan for the day includes . . .

The best part of today was . . .

Today I am grateful for . . .

Mood tracker

DAY 33

My intentions for the day are . . .

Sleep quality:

Hours of sleep:

Today I ate . . .

Today's activities will be:

My self-care plan for the day includes . . .

The best part of today was . . .

Today I am grateful for . . .

Mood tracker

DAY 34

My intentions for the day are . . .

Sleep quality:

Hours of sleep:

Today I ate . . .

Today's activities will be:

My self-care plan for the day includes . . .

The best part of today was . . .

Today I am grateful for . . .

Mood tracker

DAY 35

My intentions for the day are . . .

Sleep quality:

Hours of sleep:

Today I ate . . .

Today's activities will be:

My self-care plan for the day includes . . .

The best part of today was . . .

Today I am grateful for . . .

Mood tracker

DAY 36

My intentions for the day are . . .

Sleep quality:

Hours of sleep:

Today's activities will be:

Today I ate . . .

My self-care plan for the day includes . . .

The best part of today was . . .

Today I am grateful for . . .

Mood tracker

DAY 37

My intentions for the day are . . .

Sleep quality:

Today's activities will be:

Hours of sleep:

Today I ate . . .

My self-care plan for the day includes . . .

The best part of today was . . .

Today I am grateful for . . .

Mood tracker

DAY 38

My intentions for the day are . . .

Sleep quality:

Hours of sleep:

Today I ate . . .

Today's activities will be:

My self-care plan for the day includes . . .

The best part of today was . . .

Today I am grateful for . . .

Mood tracker

DAY 39

My intentions for the day are . . .

Sleep quality:

Hours of sleep:

Today I ate . . .

Today's activities will be:

My self-care plan for the day includes . . .

The best part of today was . . .

Today I am grateful for . . .

Mood tracker

DAY 40

My intentions for the day are . . .

Sleep quality:

Hours of sleep:

Today I ate . . .

Today's activities will be:

My self-care plan for the day includes . . .

The best part of today was . . .

Today I am grateful for . . .

Mood tracker

DAY 41

My intentions for the day are . . .

Sleep quality:

Hours of sleep:

Today I ate . . .

Today's activities will be:

My self-care plan for the day includes . . .

The best part of today was . . .

Today I am grateful for . . .

Mood tracker

DAY 42

My intentions for the day are . . .

Sleep quality:

Hours of sleep:

Today's activities will be:

Today I ate . . .

My self-care plan for the day includes . . .

The best part of today was . . .

Today I am grateful for . . .

Mood tracker

DAY 43

My intentions for the day are . . .

Sleep quality:

Hours of sleep:

Today's activities will be:

Today I ate . . .

My self-care plan for the day includes . . .

The best part of today was . . .

Today I am grateful for . . .

Mood tracker

DAY 44

My intentions for the day are . . .

Sleep quality:

Today's activities will be:

Hours of sleep:

Today I ate . . .

My self-care plan for the day includes . . .

The best part of today was . . .

Today I am grateful for . . .

Mood tracker

DAY 45

My intentions for the day are . . .

Sleep quality:

Hours of sleep:

Today's activities will be:

Today I ate . . .

My self-care plan for the day includes . . .

The best part of today was . . .

Today I am grateful for . . .

Mood tracker

DAY 46

My intentions for the day are . . .

Sleep quality:

Hours of sleep:

Today I ate . . .

Today's activities will be:

My self-care plan for the day includes . . .

The best part of today was . . .

Today I am grateful for . . .

Mood tracker

DAY 47

My intentions for the day are . . .

Sleep quality:

Today's activities will be:

Hours of sleep:

Today I ate . . .

My self-care plan for the day includes . . .

The best part of today was . . .

Today I am grateful for . . .

Mood tracker

DAY 48

My intentions for the day are . . .

Sleep quality:

Today's activities will be:

Hours of sleep:

Today I ate . . .

My self-care plan for the day includes . . .

The best part of today was . . .

Today I am grateful for . . .

Mood tracker

DAY 49

My intentions for the day are . . .

Sleep quality:

Hours of sleep:

Today I ate . . .

Today's activities will be:

My self-care plan for the day includes . . .

The best part of today was . . .

Today I am grateful for . . .

Mood tracker

DAY 50

My intentions for the day are . . .

Sleep quality:

Hours of sleep:

Today I ate . . .

Today's activities will be:

My self-care plan for the day includes . . .

The best part of today was . . .

Today I am grateful for . . .

Mood tracker

DAY 51

My intentions for the day are . . .

Sleep quality:

Hours of sleep:

Today I ate . . .

Today's activities will be:

My self-care plan for the day includes . . .

The best part of today was . . .

Today I am grateful for . . .

Mood tracker

DAY 52

My intentions for the day are . . .

Sleep quality:

Today's activities will be:

Hours of sleep:

Today I ate . . .

My self-care plan for the day includes . . .

The best part of today was . . .

Today I am grateful for . . .

Mood tracker

DAY 53

My intentions for the day are . . .

Sleep quality:

Hours of sleep:

Today I ate . . .

Today's activities will be:

My self-care plan for the day includes . . .

The best part of today was . . .

Today I am grateful for . . .

Mood tracker

DAY 54

My intentions for the day are . . .

Sleep quality:

Today's activities will be:

Hours of sleep:

Today I ate . . .

My self-care plan for the day includes . . .

The best part of today was . . .

Today I am grateful for . . .

Mood tracker

DAY 55

My intentions for the day are . . .

Sleep quality:

Hours of sleep:

Today I ate . . .

Today's activities will be:

My self-care plan for the day includes . . .

The best part of today was . . .

Today I am grateful for . . .

Mood tracker

DAY 56

My intentions for the day are . . .

Sleep quality:

Hours of sleep:

Today's activities will be:

Today I ate . . .

My self-care plan for the day includes . . .

The best part of today was . . .

Today I am grateful for . . .

Mood tracker

DAY 57

My intentions for the day are . . .

Sleep quality:

Today's activities will be:

Hours of sleep:

Today I ate . . .

My self-care plan for the day includes . . .

The best part of today was . . .

Today I am grateful for . . .

Mood tracker

DAY 58

My intentions for the day are . . .

Sleep quality:

Hours of sleep:

Today I ate . . .

Today's activities will be:

My self-care plan for the day includes . . .

The best part of today was . . .

Today I am grateful for . . .

Mood tracker

DAY 59

My intentions for the day are . . .

Sleep quality:

Hours of sleep:

Today I ate . . .

Today's activities will be:

My self-care plan for the day includes . . .

The best part of today was . . .

Today I am grateful for . . .

Mood tracker

DAY 60

My intentions for the day are . . .

Sleep quality:

Hours of sleep:

Today I ate . . .

Today's activities will be:

My self-care plan for the day includes . . .

The best part of today was . . .

Today I am grateful for . . .

Mood tracker

DAY 61

My intentions for the day are . . .

Sleep quality:

Hours of sleep:

Today I ate . . .

Today's activities will be:

My self-care plan for the day includes . . .

The best part of today was . . .

Today I am grateful for . . .

Mood tracker

DAY 62

My intentions for the day are . . .

Sleep quality:

Today's activities will be:

Hours of sleep:

Today I ate . . .

My self-care plan for the day includes . . .

The best part of today was . . .

Today I am grateful for . . .

Mood tracker

DAY 63

My intentions for the day are . . .

Sleep quality:

Hours of sleep:

Today's activities will be:

Today I ate . . .

My self-care plan for the day includes . . .

The best part of today was . . .

Today I am grateful for . . .

Mood tracker

DAY 64

My intentions for the day are . . .

Sleep quality:

Today's activities will be:

Hours of sleep:

Today I ate . . .

My self-care plan for the day includes . . .

The best part of today was . . .

Today I am grateful for . . .

Mood tracker

DAY 65

My intentions for the day are . . .

Sleep quality:

Today's activities will be:

Hours of sleep:

Today I ate . . .

My self-care plan for the day includes . . .

The best part of today was . . .

Today I am grateful for . . .

Mood tracker

DAY 66

My intentions for the day are . . .

Sleep quality:

Today's activities will be:

Hours of sleep:

Today I ate . . .

My self-care plan for the day includes . . .

The best part of today was . . .

Today I am grateful for . . .

Mood tracker

YOU DID IT!

CONGRATULATIONS YOU HAVE COMPLETED 66 DAYS OF JOURNALING! HOPEFULLY THIS IS NOW A HABIT THAT YOU WILL CONTINUE INDEFINITELY. LET'S NOW TAKE SOME TIME TO REFLECT ON HOW THINGS WENT . . .

What did you learn?

Write down the most valuable lesson that you have learned while completing this book.

WHAT SURPRISED YOU?

WHAT WERE YOU THE MOST SURPRISED ABOUT WHEN YOU BEGAN REALLY THINKING ABOUT SELF-CARE?

HAVE YOU CHANGED FOR THE BETTER?

HOW HAS THIS JOURNAL CHANGED YOU?
HOW DO YOU FEEL NOW?

MAKE A COMMITMENT

WRITE DOWN HOW YOU ARE GOING TO ENSURE THAT YOU CONTINUE TO LOOK AFTER YOUR WELLBEING?

DEAR FUTURE ME . . .

WRITE A LETTER TO YOUR FUTURE SELF THAT YOU CAN READ IF YOU EVER FALL BACK INTO BAD HABITS AND STOP TAKING CARE OF YOURSELF